Pastoral Care
& Counselling

D1514324

Ethics in Practice Series

Ethics in Practice edited by Tim Bond is a series of short, practical guides to ethical issues which confront counsellors, psychotherapists and other professionals every day. Suitable for both students and practitioners, the books are designed to give a clearer understanding of issues which are often considered complex and contentious.

Books in the series:

Therapy with Children
Debbie Daniels and Peter Jenkins

Pastoral Care & Counselling
Gordon Lynch

Legal Issues in Counselling & Psychotherapy
Peter Jenkins

Pastoral Care & Counselling

This book, focusing as it does on the ethics underpinning any pastoral care or counselling relationship, was a real joy to read being well-written, engaging and thought provoking. Drawing on a rich variety of ethical dilemmas and presenting some complex ethical thinking in a disarmingly simple way, Gordon Lynch invites us to engage more deeply with our own ethical nature. We are encouraged to discover what the good life means to us and how this impacts on pastoral encounters. This book does not give us any easy ethical answers, instead it invites us to reflect more deeply on our own ethical viewpoint and how this can inform our pastoral work with clients. I wholeheartedly recommend this book to anyone involved in pastoral care and counselling.

Dr William West, Senior Lecturer in Counselling, University of Manchester

Pastoral Care & Counselling

Gordon Lynch

SAGE Publications
London • Thousand Oaks • New Delhi

This book is dedicated to all of those who have helped me
get to the point where I could write it, in particular to
Mum and Dad, and to Rosalyn

SAGE Publications Ltd
6 Bonhill Street
London EC2A 4PU

SAGE Publications Inc
2455 Teller Road
Thousand Oaks, California 91320

SAGE Publications India Pvt Ltd
32, M-Block Market
Greater Kailash - I
New Delhi 110 048

British Library Cataloguing in Publication data

A catalogue record for this book is available
from the British Library

ISBN 0 7619 7096 7
ISBN 0 7619 7097 5 (pbk)

Library of Congress Control Number: 2002102292

Typeset by C&M Digitals (P) Ltd., Chennai, India
Printed in Great Britain by TJ International Ltd, Padstow, Cornwall

Contents

Foreword

It is a privilege and a pleasure to write a foreword to this book. Gordon Lynch is a talented counsellor and pastoral theologian. I very much appreciate being given the opportunity to commend this useful, highly original, and practical contribution to thinking about ethics, values and pastoral practice.

I generally skip book forewords and go on to the main text. I have no hesitation in commending this as an appropriate response here – there is so much to look forward to in the pages that follow. However, for inveterate foreword readers, let me share some of the reasons why I think this is a book that is very well worth reading and how I think it engages with important contemporary debates and issues in pastoral care and counselling.

Perhaps the most important thing about this volume from the reader's viewpoint is that it is beautifully, clearly written. This is a text for those who are not experts in ethics or moral reflection. It provides a lucid introduction to the field. Even if you have never thought about ethics and values before, you will find that you are introduced to complex concepts in a totally comprehensible way. Gordon Lynch relates heavyweight philosophical thinkers such as Levinas and Gramsci to moral reflections about pastoral practice. He discusses ideas such as 'hegemony' and 'theories in use'. But such is the deftness with which these thinkers and concepts are introduced and then exemplified, that readers will not suppose that they were ever difficult in the first place. The author has a rare gift for explanation and relational thinking. This should make even the least intellectual pastoral carer a fully fledged postmodern thinker, without leaving any furrows on the brow. At all points ideas are related to real case studies. Theory is never allowed to become detached from practice.

This book is an introductory text. However, it is also highly original in its approach to thinking about ethics in pastoral practice. Often, ethical approaches to pastoral care consist of naming and labelling moral dilemmas, or of elaborate casuistry along the lines of 'What should be done here?'. Frequently, this kind of approach is compounded by the use of technical and off-putting moral terms such as deontology, utilitarianism, aretaic approaches etc. The trouble here is that the wood gets lost in the trees; ethical or moral reflection becomes a matter of dissecting 'problem' situations using the tools of procedural ethics. Lynch rises above this, providing a bigger vision of moral reflection that dovetails beautifully with the broader concept of reflective practice.

Central to Lynch's model for moral reflective practice is the notion of promoting the good life. This is a positive, future-oriented view of existence to which pastoral care and counselling should contribute. The idea of placing moral reflection in the context of trying to promote human flourishing in its widest sense has a long history in Christian theology. It is particularly prominent within Catholic Thomist philosophy – heavily influenced by Aristotelian thinking – that originated with St Thomas Aquinas in the twelfth century. Unfortunately, it has often got lost in the problem-solving, rational, instrumental, and fragmentary approach that frequently characterises thought about care today. Often, various kinds of pastoral care and counselling have not borne witness to the important questions of ultimate vision and purpose that should validate or question all kinds of activity. Questions such as, where are human beings going, what will assist their progress, and how might they be helped to get there?

So far, so abstract and uncritical perhaps. But Lynch never ducks difficult questions about theory or practice. He discusses at length whether it is possible to have a single view of 'the good life' in the light of issues of cultural relativism and postmodern pluralism. One of the real strengths of the book is that it fully recognises that in different cultures the good life may mean something other than what it does in the West. This provides a powerful, if implicit, critique of much of the thinking that has gone into Western ethical codes of counselling which seem to prize individual autonomy over community and belonging. It seems to me that most theorists of ethics and counselling have not yet begun to realise the scope and limits of the ethical discourse of the Western capitalist 'tribe'. Lynch is way out in front; his book is therefore relevant to those involved in care and counselling who would in no sense see themselves as involved in religion or pastoral work.

The model and technique of reflecting and identifying basic values and implicit views of the good life that surface in all caring encounters is also original and relevant beyond the world of pastoral care. Lynch's challenge is that we should all become aware of our inevitable action guiding visions and enactments of the good life in our caring encounters. He not only provides the rationale for this thoughtful, reflective approach, but also the techniques, questions and examples that will allow us to do this critical work for ourselves.

Pastoral Care & Counselling is not so much a 'how to do it' book, as a 'how to think and reflect upon it' work. Concrete questions about the nature and value of professional codes, the importance of boundaries in caring relationships, the place of friendship and other matters are dealt with in depth. However, the book's real challenge to its readers is to ask them to think more widely and deeply about the nature of care and caring within the context of a broad vision of human flourishing. Thus it adds theory and substance to the art of reflective practice. Whether reflection on values and assumptions changes practice is a moot point. But if people are not aware of their fundamental beliefs and motivating principles and guidelines, then there will be little possibility of criticising or changing them.

I do have some reservations about Lynch's use of concepts such as 'values' which seem somewhat vague. And I personally prefer the notion of human flourishing to that of the good life. This allows for a greater variety of understanding that is truer to the plurality of human well being; different flowers in a garden grow and flourish in different ways. Furthermore, I believe that overtly religious and theological traditions, as well as insights from Aristotelian philosophy, should be more actively involved in the shaping of values and ethics in pastoral care and counselling – else why should this activity be called pastoral?

However, these are minor points. The important thing about this book is that it will help newcomers and experienced practitioners to analyse and expand their awareness of the moral dimensions of their reflective practice in a positive, novel way. It will allow them to situate their everyday assumptions and actions within a broader view of human potential. And it is a very good read which will leave them feeling ready to learn more. I feel sure that *Pastoral Care & Counselling* will be enjoyed and profited from by those who are lucky enough to have access to it.

Stephen Pattison
Cardiff University

Introduction

Pastoral practice is by its very nature an inter-disciplinary activity. Theology, biblical studies, philosophy, psychology, sociology, anthropology, cultural studies and social and economic theory, all have an important role to play in helping us to think about the assumptions, aims and methods of pastoral practice. By comparison, some disciplines have been mined more extensively than others as resources for reflecting on pastoral practice. A range of writers have therefore explored the relevance of theological concepts and metaphors for pastoral work (see, for example, Oden, 1984; Gerkin, 1991; Hurding, 1998). Counselling psychology has also been explored in some depth as a source of theories and methods for pastoral work (see, for example, Clinebell, 1984; Jacobs, 1993). A growing literature is also beginning to consider the relevance of social theory for understanding and critiquing pastoral work (see, for example, Pattison, 1994; Furniss, 1995).

Ethics, by contrast, is one of those disciplines whose relevance to pastoral practice has not been considered in such depth. Whilst a few texts have been written on this subject over the past twenty five years (for example, Browning, 1983; Noyce, 1989; Atkinson, 1994; Miles, 1999), the literature on ethics and pastoral practice remains relatively undeveloped, particularly amongst writers in the United Kingdom.

The fundamental aim of this book is therefore to contribute to an understanding of why ethics and moral reflection are relevant and important to the theory and practice of pastoral care. My interest in writing this book has not been to produce a highly theoretical or abstract overview of the nature of ethics as a discipline that pastoral practitioners then have to try to relate to their day-to-day experience. Nor have I wanted to take a narrow approach to this subject and simply focus on the 'moral dilemmas' or issues of professional ethics that pastoral workers encounter (although these will also be discussed later in the book). Rather my aim here is to argue that all pastoral practice is value-based and that, as such, moral reflection is fundamentally important to the process of thinking about what pastoral practitioners do and what they seek to achieve through their work. In producing this book, my hope is that I am developing a resource that will help pastoral carers and coun-sellors to think critically about the values that are already influencing their practice and about the different ways in which moral reflection can be relevant to their work.

As you read this, you will probably become increasingly aware that generally I am not trying to offer anything like final answers to the various moral questions and issues that arise in relation to pastoral work. Indeed my concern in writing this book is primarily to provide a framework for *reflection*; a way of thinking about pastoral practice that helps us to analyse the different ways in which values and ethics are relevant to it. This approach reflects my belief that seeking to impose clear and rigid ethical answers on the day-to-day situations we encounter is unlikely to be productive, either for ourselves or for those with whom we work. Rather, I believe it is more important that pastoral workers develop skills of reflection – of being able to identify and think through the key issues raised by their practice – as such skills are essential for thoughtful negotiation of the rough and complex terrain of our day-to-day experience.

Theory has an important role to play in assisting such reflection, and the framework for thinking about pastoral practice that I present in this book is influenced by a particular range of theoretical ideas. I have chosen not to discuss these theoretical influences at length in the main text of the book itself, as I suspect that this would tend to be of interest more to readers who already have considerable experience of ideas and debates in the field of ethics. For readers with some familiarity with the discipline of ethics, though, it will be clear that part of my influence is from a broadly Aristotelian tradition that focuses on the importance of the good life, wisdom, friendship and virtue rather than beginning with questions about how we respond to specific 'moral dilemmas'. Although I am familiar with a wider range of Aristotelian literature, I have been primarily influenced by the work of the theological ethicist Stanley Hauerwas (1981, 1983, 2001). Whilst I would not always share the ethical conclusions that he reaches, I have been very much shaped by Hauerwas' broader ethical approach. Some readers may also pick up on the fact that I am not particularly concerned to argue on theoretical grounds for the truth of many of the ideas that I present. This reflects another postmodern strand of influence on my thought in which I share the scepticism of writers such as Kenneth Gergen (1994) and Richard Rorty (1999) about the possibility of finding objective ways of demonstrating the truth of our ideas. Instead, I am more concerned in my work to develop ideas and ways of thinking that may be *useful* for us in the situations in which we find ourselves, rather than becoming bogged down in ultimately irresolvable arguments about *truthfulness* (see Lynch, 1999a).

My guess, though, is that most readers of this book are unlikely to be immediately curious about these more theoretical influences and assumptions, and will be more interested in what I have to say about how ethics and moral reflection relates to pastoral practice. Indeed it is with such readers in mind that I have written this book. As a consequence,

I have tried to make frequent reference to case material as a basis and focus for my discussion. In doing so, my hope is that I will have demonstrated in fairly concrete ways how values and moral reflection are relevant and important to practice.

Whilst I think it is a strength of this book, some readers may find the breadth of my approach and style somewhat frustrating. In particular, some readers may wish that I would use explicitly religious or theological language more often. Or to put it more simply, that I would say more about how God relates to all of these questions and issues. I have been reluctant to be more explicitly theological in this book for two reasons. First, although in the past I have been significantly formed by my membership of the Christian Church, I find myself at a point in my life at present where I would not choose to identify with any one religious faith or institution. Whilst the approach in this book inevitably reflects my own beliefs and commitments, these beliefs and commitments are not such that I would currently want to use orthodox theological language to express them. The relative absence of traditional theological language in this book thus reflects my own choice about how I want to present my ideas at this time. Second, my reluctance to use concepts or symbols from a specific faith tradition reflects my hope that the model for moral reflection presented in this book is one that can be inclusive for practitioners from a range of different religious backgrounds. My belief is that the kind of questions that I am raising here are relevant regardless of whether one's religious commitment is Buddhist, Christian, Hindu, Jewish, Muslim or Sikh. In practice, where I do use particular examples of religious language, ritual, symbol or story in this book, I generally take them from the Christian tradition, as this is the tradition with which I am most familiar. My hope, though, is that whatever your particular religious belief or affiliation, you will find something useful in the approach to moral reflection that I adopt in the coming chapters.

Having made some general comments about the aims, assumptions and style of the book, I will now give a brief overview of the content of what is to come. In Chapter 1, I introduce the argument at the heart of this book, namely that all pastoral practice is influenced by the pastoral worker's values and that careful reflection on the values that shape pastoral practice is thus important. I go on to discuss the significance of the pastoral worker's 'vision of the good life' for their understanding of the aims and methods of their work. Finally I raise a series of questions that can be asked about a pastoral worker's understanding of the good life that will provide the structure for the remaining chapters.

In Chapter 2, I pick up the first of the questions raised at the end of the previous chapter, that is the issue of how pastoral carers and counsellors can identify their own particular vision of the good life. I argue that the process of identifying our values is not a straightforward one, partly because we are not automatically aware of them, partly because our deeply-held cultural values can seem too 'natural' or 'obvious' for us to see them as values, and partly because our personal values are not always consistent. I suggest that there are a range of ways in which we can become more aware of our values. A close analysis of particular instances of pastoral practice that we have engaged in – using transcripts or tape recordings – can make us more aware of value judgments that we have made with the people that we are working with. Engaging with descriptions of pastoral practice from cultures different to our own can also make us more aware of the values that tend to be dominant in our own particular cultural context. Furthermore identifying 'stories of the good life' that are important to us, can help us articulate our values, even when we hold values that may contradict each other at times.

In Chapter 3, I move on to more general questions about how we might approach the question of how adequate our particular vision of the good life is. Referring to the work of Don Browning, I summarise four levels of reflection that Browning identifies that we can bring to this general ethical question, and note the importance of experience, reason and revelation as resources for pastoral reflection on the nature of the good life. I then explore the question of whether it is possible or desirable to attempt to give a single, clear definition of the good life. I suggest that it is important to recognise the provisional and local nature of any definition of the good life that we construct, whilst remaining clear that not all definitions of the good life are equally acceptable. Finally I suggest two concepts that I believe represent important elements for adequate notions of the good life – a proper regard for the 'Other' and a proper regard for personal authenticity.

In Chapters 4 to 7, I then explore how moral reflection is relevant to different dimensions of the pastoral encounter. In Chapter 4, I focus on the social and institutional context of the pastoral encounter and argue that moral reflection on pastoral practice needs to involve reflection on what social or institutional factors impede an experience of the good life. Two case examples form the central focus of this chapter. The first case study concerns an instance of domestic violence and leads into an exploration of the relationship between domestic violence and wider patriarchal concepts and assumptions within society. The second involves the process of planning an elderly patient's discharge from hospital and opens up discussion of the significance of ageism and other institutional factors in limiting this man's experience of the good life.

In Chapter 5, the focus shifts to the boundaries of the pastoral encounter. I argue that appropriate boundaries are important to protect those who seek pastoral care, and that the notion of the 'therapeutic frame' can at least begin to help us to ask questions about what kinds of boundaries are important for pastoral relationships. The chapter concludes with a discussion of the relative importance of pastoral workers developing their own ability to reflect on how to structure their pastoral relationships and on the creation of codes of practice which provide pastoral workers with a framework for thinking about their practice.

In Chapter 6, an emphasis is placed on the importance of the interpersonal qualities of the pastoral relationship. The central question raised here is, therefore, what kind of interpersonal qualities need to be present in the pastoral encounter to promote an experience of the good life. I suggest that Aristotle's idea of a 'friendship of virtue' is a helpful one for thinking about the qualities of good pastoral relationships. Drawing on the work of Alistair Campbell, I thus suggest that the ideal pastoral relationship could be seen as a 'moderated friendship' in which those involved show mutual regard and understanding for each other in ways that are appropriate to their respective roles.

Finally, in Chapter 7, I look at the importance of moral reflection in relation to the discussion of moral dilemmas. Using the example of a young man raising questions about the expression of his gay sexuality, I note the different styles of moral thinking associated with the 'deontological' and 'consequentialist' approaches to ethics. I suggest that, in practice, moral reflection is often more complicated and messy than these two abstract approaches to it suggest. I summarise a framework for thinking about moral dilemmas which has been developed by Rebekah Miles (1999) and explore the potential value of her model. This leads into a further discussion about how pastoral practitioners can appropriately make their own values explicit in pastoral conversations. Finally, I suggest that identifying and responding to 'moral dilemmas' is not simply a process of conscious, rational reflection, but that this process will be influenced by our own moral character and the particular virtues that we have developed. Moral reflection in relation to pastoral practice thus goes beyond thinking about particular 'moral dilemmas' to raising wider questions about what kind of moral character we should aspire to and what resources help us to develop that character.

In writing this book, I am conscious of the debt that I owe to a number of people who have helped me to develop this approach and these ideas. First, I must thank Tim Bond, as series editor, and Alison Poyner at Sage, who have both given me valuable editorial support and encouragement. I must also thank the Communications Office of the Diocese of Oxford for granting me permission to use extracts from that diocese's *Code of Ministerial Conduct*.

I have been fortunate to have had the opportunity of exploring many of the ideas in this book with students on the Diploma and Masters' programmes in Pastoral Studies in the Department of Theology at Birmingham University. My ideas here have been enriched by my experience of working alongside people on those programmes who come from a highly diverse range of theological and cultural backgrounds. I have also benefitted from discussing ideas with other research students and with the open seminar for Pastoral Studies in my department. Paul Grace very kindly read through the draft of this book and made valuable suggestions that helped me to clarify its content, and I am grateful to him for our conversations about the book. I am particularly grateful to three people who, over the past years, have been significant academic mentors for me. Emmanuel Lartey, who supervised my PhD, provided me with an inspirational example of how to engage in critical practical theological reflection that engages both with the personal and the social. John McLeod gave me important encouragement about the usefulness of the idea of the 'good life' and I have benefitted greatly from my conversations with him on this and wider issues of therapeutic practice. To Stephen Pattison I owe the specific debt of gratitude of writing the Foreword to this book. I also owe Stephen Pattison a much more general debt, as my conversations with him and exposure to his writing have undoubtedly been one of the most formative influences on the development of my thinking over the past few years (as a casual glance at the Bibliography will demonstrate).

I am grateful to everyone who has contributed to the process by which this book, and the ideas within it, have been developed. I hope that in the end it will make some contribution to the on-going process of thinking about what it means to live well in the world and to encourage further discussion about how pastoral practice can help to promote human well-being.

Gordon Lynch
Department of Theology
University of Birmingham

1

The significance of values & moral reflection for pastoral care & counselling

Over the past twenty years or so, an increasing number of writers have been exploring the subject of ethics in relation to pastoral care and counselling. Some writers have approached this area by trying to give some guidance to pastoral practitioners about how they can work constructively with people who are facing moral dilemmas, such as whether they should seek a divorce from their spouse or terminate a pregnancy. Other writers have thought about the 'professional' ethics of pastoral work, and have sought to explore the pastoral significance of principles such as confidentiality and the avoidance of abuse of clients. A third emphasis – and one perhaps less commonly heard than the other two – argues that all pastoral practice is shaped by the pastoral carer's values and that there is a need for moral reflection in relation to all forms of pastoral work.

It is important, at the outset of this book, to clarify what approach I will be taking to this subject. Helping people to work through moral dilemmas and thinking about what it means to act in an ethical and competent way are both important issues for pastoral workers and each of them will be explored in more detail later in the book. In my view, though, if we are to get a proper sense of the significance of ethics for pastoral care and counselling, it is important to recognise the fundamental role that values play in all forms of pastoral practice. In this opening chapter, then, I will be taking time to illustrate the notion that pastoral practice is essentially value-based and, more specifically, to suggest that the work of pastoral carers and counsellors is inspired by their vision of the good life.

Values, Moral Reflection and Pastoral Practice

What grounds are there for suggesting that all pastoral practice is inspired, in some way, by the pastoral worker's values? Let me try to illustrate this notion through the following case example:

Susan has worked as a voluntary chaplaincy assistant for a number of years at a large city hospital. She goes into the hospital twice a week, once to help with the Sunday morning service and the other day to visit patients on one of the medical wards in the hospital. During one of her visits to the ward, Susan spent time talking with Mr Davis, an elderly man who had been admitted to hospital with a severe chest infection. As she talked with Mr Davis, he became tearful and told her that he had lived on his own for six years since the death of his wife. Although he could generally cope on his own with practical tasks, he found the loneliness of being by himself much harder to cope with. His daughter would visit him two or three times a month, but lived some distance away, and apart from going out to the shops he would not see much of other people.

Susan listened empathically as Mr Davis talked about his loneliness. After talking together for a while, she mentioned to him that she knew that there was a church lunch club that met in his area and she could pass his name on to the organiser of that group. When Susan mentioned the club, Mr Davis became a bit more reticent and said that he would think about it. Susan tried to encourage him to go along by telling him that the club was friendly and not particularly religious, if that was something that he found off-putting. Mr Davis still seemed unsure, though, and said that Susan could give him the details of the lunch club if she liked, and he would think about it. Susan wrote the details down for him, and shortly afterwards she and Mr Davis said their goodbyes, with him expressing his gratitude to her for listening to him.

On leaving the ward Susan thought to herself that Mr Davis still seemed anxious about the idea of the lunch club and that, if not followed up, he might not pursue it. This seemed a great shame to her as, knowing the club, she thought Mr Davis would probably fit in there very well. As Susan walked back to the chaplaincy office she wondered to herself whether she might still pass Mr Davis' details on to the lunch club organiser. The organiser could visit Mr Davis herself and tell him more about the club, and hopefully that would put any fears he had about going there to rest. Susan would go back to Mr Davis and tell him that she had passed his name on, that she hoped he wouldn't mind this and that there was no pressure for him to go to the club if he didn't want to. By the time Susan got to the office she decided that that was what she would do.

This case example is not a particularly dramatic story. If anything it is a fairly low-key interaction of a kind that a pastoral carer might even experience several times in any given day. The ordinary nature of this encounter raises the question of what values and moral reflection have to do with real, day-to-day, pastoral practice.

We may begin to recognise the significance of values for pastoral practice if we acknowledge that the way that we ourselves react to Susan's behaviour in this case reflects our own values. Some readers looking at this case will think that Susan acted in a wholly appropriate way. They might argue Mr Davis was clearly lonely and socially isolated, and regretted his lack of regular contact with other people. By deciding to refer him on, Susan may have taken an important first step in helping Mr Davis become more socially connected to other people. Other readers, however, may feel quite uncomfortable with Susan's actions. They might point out that Mr Davis made his wishes quite clear to her about how he wished to proceed with the idea of the lunch club, and her decision to go against his wishes could be seen as patronising and disempowering. At the heart of these differing interpretations of the case lie different values about what it means to live well. If one places a high value on friendship and the experience of belonging with other people, then Susan's pro-active approach could be seen as good in terms of trying to overcome Mr Davis' social isolation. If, on the other hand, one believes that the ability to act as an autonomous individual is an essential part of what it means to live well, then Susan's action could be seen as bad because it undermined Mr Davis' ability to make decisions in his own right.

If the way that we respond to this case study reflects our own values, then it may be reasonable to go on to suggest that the way Susan acted in this case reflected her particular beliefs about what is valuable in life. All forms of therapeutic practice, whether psychiatry, social work, counselling or pastoral care, seek to alleviate human suffering and deprivation and seek to promote human well-being. Underlying such therapeutic practices are ideas about what constitutes human suffering and well-being, and these ideas are essentially value-statements about what is important about life. Thus (as we shall see in the next chapter) a pastoral practitioner working in the context of traditional African culture will be likely to see involvement in the extended family and the wider community as an important part of human well-being. In their practice they will therefore tend to seek to reconcile individuals to their communities. By contrast, many pastoral carers working in Western society will be more influenced by Western ideas about the significance of the individual, and may be more likely to seek to promote individual development and self-expression through their work. Even within ostensibly scientific theories of therapeutic practice (such as theories of counselling and psychotherapy) lie value-statements about what it means to live well. Psychodynamic theories (certainly more traditional Freudian approaches) have tended, like the Greek Stoics, to emphasise the importance of the recognition and acceptance of the realities of human existence rather than the struggle against it (Gellner, 1985). Humanistic approaches, such as person-centred counselling, have tended on the other hand to value self-expression, authenticity and creativity as important aspects of what it means to be human. All therapeutic practice can

therefore be seen to be influenced by underlying ideas or values about what it means to live well. In choosing the course of action that she did, Susan demonstrated that she saw connection with others to be more important than personal autonomy, and our degree of sympathy with Susan's practice will probably reflect how closely her notion of what is valuable in life resembles our own.

Values therefore provide the compass bearings by which we make sense of and judge pastoral practice. Consciously or unconsciously, they provide a framework by which pastoral workers decide what is the most appropriate, helpful and therapeutic way in which they can work with the people that they encounter.

If values are so significant in shaping the way that pastoral carers and counsellors think about their work, then it seems reasonable to claim that 'ethics' or 'moral reflection' (the practice of thinking critically about one's values and current context) is also of fundamental importance for pastoral work. Stephen Pattison makes the case for moral reflection in relation to pastoral work in the following way:

> It is so much easier to get on with the job of caring for people than to try and unravel the knots which ethical considerations bring to the fore. Easy, but dangerous. For the fact is that where pastoral care ignores ethics it is in peril of promoting values or dealing in practices which, on reflection, it might find rather undesirable, dubious or harmful. All human activities have ethical aspects and consequences. These may be implicit and unconscious or conscious and explicit. In the latter case they can be examined and changed; in the former, there is always the possibility that the wrong aims, methods and tools may be unwittingly promoted to the detriment of those who care, as well as those who are cared for. (Pattison, 1988: 35).

Moral reflection can therefore enable pastoral practitioners to be more aware of the values that shape their practice. In the case discussed above, if Susan reflected on the values guiding her practice she might decide to modify her practice in a way that gave greater respect to Mr Davis' autonomy. Equally, though, Susan might decide on the basis of such reflection that it was indeed appropriate to act in a way that valued social connectedness over individual autonomy. The usefulness of such reflection, however, is that it would make Susan a more self-aware practitioner and that, as such, she would be more able to make conscious and thoughtful decisions about her practice. Clearly being thoughtful about one's practice does not guarantee that one will work in a way that does actually promote human wellbeing. It is a reasonable (albeit modest) claim, though, that reflective, thoughtful practice is more likely to be open to on-going critical scrutiny than practice which is based on unconscious or assumed values.[1]

Reflection on one's values can therefore be seen as an important task for anyone involved in therapeutic work. Since the late 1970s, however, a number of writers have argued that there is a particularly urgent need for such reflection amongst pastoral carers in Western society. Various explanations have been advanced for why Western pastoral practitioners may have found it difficult to recognise and reflect upon the values that are implicit in their work. Don Browning (1983), for example, has argued that pastoral practitioners whose work is heavily influenced by secular models of counselling and psychotherapy may tend to interpret their work as having a scientific, psychological basis rather than a moral one. Tom Oden (1984) similarly sees the influence of secular (ostensibly scientific) psychotherapies on pastoral practice as diminishing pastoral practitioners' ability to think about the moral and theological dimensions of their work. This factor is likely to be more true of pastoral practitioners in the United States, however, than in Britain where the influence of secular models of counselling and psychotherapy on pastoral practice has generally been less strong.

Another reason why pastoral workers may find it difficult to think about their work in terms of values, is the desire of many pastoral workers to avoid 'moralism' in their practice. Moralism could be defined as the imposition of a set of values upon a group or individual in a way that does not take any account of their particular experiences or circumstances. Moralism can therefore be seen as a morally judgmental approach to human interaction, in which a person makes critical and insensitive judgments of others' lives in a way that alienates or shames them, rather than promoting a constructive conversation with them. It seems reasonable to claim that some individuals and groups have experienced, and continue to experience, moralistic statements and actions from religious workers and organisations. It also seems reasonable to say that moralism is something to be avoided if we are genuinely interested in promoting constructive, mature and healthy human relationships. The desire to avoid moralism in pastoral practice can therefore be welcomed as part of the increasing awareness that pastoral care and counselling has the potential to be an abusive and damaging experience for those who receive it (Layzell, 1999).

Some writers would claim, however, that in seeking to avoid moralism, many pastoral practitioners have been tempted to neglect thinking about the moral dimension of their work altogether (see, for example, Pattison; 1988: 33f.). As Rebekah Miles (1999: 3) puts it, 'many pastors today hesitate to make moral judgments at all for fear of giving offense, hurting someone's feelings, or becoming "judgmental"'. This can leave pastoral workers in what Miles refers to as the 'muddled middle', caught between a sense that values and ethics are important for pastoral practice and a concern that to embody an active moral stance in their work will be damaging to those for whom they care. Some practitioners may seek to deal with this bind by thinking about their practice as being in some sense 'value-free'. Writers such as Don Browning and Tom Oden have argued, however, that there can never be a moral vacuum at the heart of one's pastoral practice. If pastoral carers aspire to be value free in their work, Browning and Oden suggest that in practice their work tends to be informed by the dominant cultural values of the day, which in the case of contemporary Western society means hedonism, personal autonomy and self-fulfilment.

A key assumption that I bring to this book is that it is possible for pastoral practitioners to reflect on, and make conscious decisions about, the values that inform their practice in a way that does not degenerate into moralism. Within the book as a whole I will argue that pastoral carers' and counsellors' work is fundamentally informed by their *vision of the good life*. Furthermore I will argue that pastoral practitioners will be better placed to promote human well-being through their work if they reflect on the adequacy of their vision of the good life and on the significance of it for different facets of the pastoral encounter. These ideas need to be explained and justified in more detail, and will be expanded upon throughout the whole of the book. In the remainder of this chapter, I will examine the significance of the concept of the good life for pastoral practitioners and introduce some broad questions that can encourage pastoral workers to think critically about the values that inform their practice.

The Good Life

In everyday speech, the term 'the good life' does not have particularly rich connotations. Indeed, in contemporary culture, 'the good life' is probably most commonly seen as something that someone is able to enjoy once they have won the National Lottery. However, reflecting about the nature of the good life has been an important part of Western culture for at least the past two and a half millennia. Key thinkers in classical Greek philosophy such as Aristotle and the Stoic philosophers were preoccupied with what kind of life we should seek to live (Arrington, 1999). In subsequent centuries, a range of philosophical and theological thinkers such as Cicero (1971), Aquinas (Porter, 1994) and Rousseau (Cooper, 1999) were similarly concerned with the question of what it means to live well.

Definitions of the good life have often consisted of two different, though often connected, elements (Smith, 1980). First, a vision of the good life will often involve an understanding of what it means to live happily or to live well. This is the sense of the good life as a life, for example, of being 'healthy, wealthy, and wise.' This element of the good life thus involves an understanding of what 'non-moral' or 'pre-moral' goods (to use formal terms from moral philosophy) we should pursue in life, whether that be material success, esteem from our peers or romantic love. The second common element of a definition of the good life is a notion of what it means to live in a way that is morally commendable. This element of the good life is thus concerned with the virtues and behaviours of a life that we can consider good, such as being honest, giving generously of our money and time, or being loyal in our relationships. Given these two different elements within a definition of the good life, the question inevitably arises about the relationship between the two. An argument commonly advanced within moral philosophy is that if one leads a life that is morally commendable, then one will experience the most happy life that one can, in one's circumstances. As Cicero (1971: 52) put it, 'in order to live a happy life the only thing we need is moral goodness.' Whilst others would wish to contest that idea, it seems clear that a full definition of the good life will need not only to set out what it means to live happily and what it means to live morally, but also what the relationship is between happiness and morality.

The quest for understanding the nature of the good life may indeed have been an important part of Western culture, but what is the significance of the notion of the good life for how we think about pastoral practice? To explore this issue further, we will think about another case scenario:

You are working as a pastoral carer in a local church congregation, and one of the members of the congregation, Laura, has arranged to see you to talk about some difficulty in her life. As Laura talks to you, it becomes clear that her main concern relates to her marriage to her husband, Rob. Both are in their mid-thirties and have been married for eight years. Laura and Rob have chosen not to have any children because they wanted to be able to concentrate on their careers. Laura and Rob's marriage started well. They met through attending the same church, and for the first two years of their marriage they very much enjoyed each other's company and seemed to be very much in love together. After those two years had passed, however, Rob got a promotion at work and spent less and less time at home. When Rob did spend time with Laura, he seemed very tired and also emotionally withdrawn from her. In the fifth year of their marriage, Laura was shocked to discover from a mutual friend that Rob had been having an affair with a work colleague for some months. She confronted him with this, and nearly ended their marriage at that point. Laura and Rob decided, though, to go to marriage counselling to see if they could manage to repair their relationship. For a while after this, their relationship seemed to improve somewhat. Rob was far more attentive and emotionally responsive to her, and Laura began to feel closer to him again. This improvement fell away, however, when Rob was promoted again within his organisation and spent even more time at his office. When Laura tried to suggest ways in which they could still spend some good time together, Rob was uninterested and said that as far as he was concerned his job came first. Their relationship has been very strained for two years now, and Laura fears that Rob may be starting another affair with a work colleague.

As Laura talks to you about her marriage it is clear that she is upset and confused. She believes that as a Christian, she should remain committed to her marriage and not seek a divorce. At the same time, though, she feels desperately unhappy in her marriage and is at the point where she thinks she may have to see her doctor for treatment for depression. She feels that she has made a great deal of effort to try to keep her marriage to Rob going, but thinks that their relationship is now so bad that it cannot be repaired. She is therefore torn between wanting to stay faithful to her marriage vows and between leaving the marriage, either to live alone or to form a close relationship with another partner who would be genuinely interested in being intimate with her.

On reading this case example, you might want to take a moment to think about how you hope Laura's situation resolves itself. Do you think it would be better if Laura stayed with Rob (even if there were no immediate prospects for the marriage improving) or do you think it would be better for her to leave the relationship and seek an intimate relationship with someone else? The way that you make sense of, and respond to, Laura's situation will reflect your own notion of the good life. Someone who holds a notion of the good life which emphasises the importance of the 'pre-moral' goods of intimacy and self-fulfillment may be more likely to see Laura leaving Rob as a better resolution of this case. Alternatively, someone who believes that the good life, in moral terms, consists of staying loyal to one's marriage vows, would be more likely to see Laura and Rob staying together as a good resolution of this situation. The particular vision of the good life that a pastoral worker holds will therefore give them some sense of what would constitute a happier ending to her story.

A vision of the good life not only provides us with an idea of how we hope Laura's situation will resolve itself, but it also influences how we interpret her current situation. When we think of Laura's story, we will not only have in mind what kind of life we hope she will experience in the future, but we may also have some ideas about what in her present situation is helping or hindering her from experiencing that kind of life. So, if we think of the good life in terms of experiencing romantic intimacy with another person then Rob could be seen as a hindrance to Laura experiencing this, since she is tied to a relationship with him in which he seems to be uninterested in being intimate with her. From this perspective, a useful resource for Laura is her awareness of her emotions about Rob, as these indicate both her desire for intimacy and her ability to detect its absence in her marriage. If, however, we see an important part of the good life as being fidelity to one's marriage vows, then the greatest threats to this for Laura at present are Rob's uncaring attitude towards her and the difficult emotions that she experiences in relation to her current rejection by Rob. From this perspective, a positive resource for Laura would be some opportunity for her and Rob to receive help in reflecting about the current state of their relationship, or, if Rob is unwilling to do this, some support for Laura to cope with this difficult period in her marriage. A vision of the good life therefore not only provides an image of the kind of life that we hope people will move towards, but also informs our current interpretation of their situation and our sense of what is helpful or harmful within it.

If a vision of the good life provides a hermeneutical framework through which pastoral practitioners make sense of the lives of those they encounter, then it seems reasonable to claim that this moral vision has direct consequences for the ways in which pastoral workers choose to engage with others. In seeking to promote human well-being, pastoral workers will naturally decide to act in ways that they believe may enable others to experience something of the good life. Thus in the case of Laura, a pastoral worker who emphasises the value of personal autonomy and fulfillment is likely to respond to her in ways that try to clarify what Laura wants, or feels is the best resolution in her situation. Alternatively, a pastoral worker who is motivated by the belief that marriage vows should be maintained as far as possible would be more likely to respond to Laura in ways that examined how she could be supported within this difficult period in her marital relationship. The notion of the good life is therefore not an abstract philosophical concept that is irrelevant to day-to-day pastoral practice. Rather, the pastoral worker's vision of the good life fundamentally shapes their hopes for the lives of those for whom they care, as well as the way that they think about and intervene within their lives.

One objection that could be raised about the argument that I am developing here is that if pastoral workers are fundamentally influenced in their practice by their vision of the good life, then this is an inappropriate state of affairs because pastoral workers should never seek to impose their values on others. This objection relates to the concern with moralism that we noted earlier in this chapter, and reflects the idea that a value-inspired pastoral practice risks being oppressive to those receiving care who do not share those values, or for whom those values may not be appropriate. Whilst the concern underlying this objection – that pastoral practice should seek to avoid being an abusive or coercive activity – is to be welcomed, the objection itself is ultimately untenable. For even if pastoral practitioners choose to 'suspend' their personal values in their work with others, and seek to work in ways that respect their clients' own values, this simply indicates that the pastoral workers' vision of the good life places a strong emphasis on personal autonomy (Lomas, 1985; Lynch, 1995). Pastoral practice uninfluenced by some form of vision of the good life is simply not possible.

Critical Reflection and Our Vision of the Good Life

So far in this chapter, then, I have suggested that all pastoral practice is informed by ideas about what is valuable in life and what it means to live well. Pastoral practice can never be 'value-free' and as a consequence it is important for pastoral workers to reflect on what values shape the way that they think about and respond to the lives and experiences of those for whom they care. In the final part of this chapter, I will suggest some broad forms that such critical reflection could take.

If we accept that pastoral practice is fundamentally guided by understandings of the good life, it seems reasonable to ask three types of question about our own practice. First, at a descriptive level, it is important to identify what particular vision of the good life we bring to our work with others? Second, at a normative level, it is important to ask whether our vision of the good life is adequate and whether it does give a proper account of human well-being and moral goodness? Third, at a practical level, it is important to ask to what extent our understanding of the good life is being promoted within different aspects of the pastoral encounter?[2] At this third level I want to suggest that there are four particular dimensions to every pastoral encounter, and that it is important to reflect on the extent to which the good life is being promoted by our work in relation to each of these four levels. The four levels of the pastoral encounter that I wish to focus attention on are:

1. *The context of the pastoral relationship:* pastoral encounters do not take place in a vacuum, but in the context of a wider society and its associated culture(s). Pastoral encounters also occur within specific social situations, and generally take place in the context of particular institutions and social organisations such as hospitals, churches or universities. It can be important for pastoral workers to reflect on the way in which the context in which their pastoral encounters take place helps or hinders the promotion of the good life through their work.

2. *The boundaries of the pastoral relationship*: pastoral practitioners, whether explicitly or implicitly, bring to their work ideas about how they should structure their contact with others, what forms of contact with others are appropriate or inappropriate, and how they should deal with issues such as confidentiality. It is again important for pastoral carers and counsellors to think about whether their approach to the boundaries of their pastoral encounters help or limit the promotion of the good life.

3. *The quality of the pastoral relationship*: each pastoral encounter is a dynamic interpersonal process between two or more people. The quality of that encounter, and the role of power in that relationship, will be significant influences on whether human well-being is promoted through it or not. Pastoral practitioners therefore need to reflect on whether the quality of the pastoral encounters that they engage in draw people towards the good life or not.

4. *The content of the pastoral conversation*: in pastoral encounters, the conversation will often focus on an individual's experience of suffering or confusion, or upon a dilemma within which they find themselves. In seeking to respond constructively to others' pain or uncertainty, it is also important for the pastoral worker to think about whether the nature of the response they make within the pastoral conversation promotes the good life or not.

Whilst I have highlighted these as being four distinct areas of the pastoral relationship, it may seem clear to many readers that these four areas of the pastoral encounter are also closely related and influenced by each other. The content of the pastoral conversation will, for example, closely reflect the quality of the pastoral relationship, and the quality of the pastoral relationship is likely to be significantly influenced by the context within which the pastoral encounter takes place. Whilst the pastoral encounter is indeed a complex whole, there can be some use in thinking about these individual parts as a focus for moral reflection in relation to our practice.

In terms of reflecting on the significance of our vision of the good life for our pastoral practice, then, I am proposing three key questions:

1. What vision of the good life influences my pastoral practice?
2. Is my vision of the good life an adequate view of human well-being and the moral life?

> 3. Is the good life promoted or hindered through the context,
>   boundaries and quality of my pastoral relationships, as well
>   as through the content of the pastoral conversations that I
>   engage in?

Summary

This chapter has sought to introduce the idea that values, and more specifically a vision of the good life, inform all types of pastoral practice. A case has been made for the importance of reflecting on the nature and adequacy of these values, and some initial questions have been presented to begin to stimulate such reflection. In the next chapter, we will begin to explore these questions further by thinking about how we can try to identify the values that inform our own practice.

Notes

1   It is open to question as to whether moral reflection can enable one to make right choices, or whether it simply enables one to be more aware of the reasons behind one's choices. Moral philosophers have disagreed on this issue with some (for example, Kant) arguing that we can know what is morally right through critical and rational reflection, and others arguing that we can never be sure of what is good and that we must simply make choices in the absence of such certainty (for example, Sartre).

2   These three levels of questioning can be seen broadly to reflect the process of practical theological reflection identified by writers such as Green, Lartey and Browning. In this process there is a movement from an initial reflection on the nature of one's current experience or practice, to a critical dialogue with other theological or non-theological sources that may generate new insights, to a reflection on the implications of this dialogue for future practice.

2

Identifying our vision of the good life

When you came to read this book on pastoral care and counselling, it may well have been the case that you expected this text to set out a range of ethical theories that could be applied to pastoral work. It will be evident from the first chapter of this book, however, that I am adopting a rather different approach to this. Rather than working from the idea that we should learn about ethical theories that we then apply to our practice, I have argued instead for the importance of our becoming critically aware of the values that already shape the work that we do. In the first chapter, I specifically suggested three kinds of question that can be raised in relation to the vision of the good life that we bring to our pastoral work. First, I identified a *descriptive* level of reflection that seeks to identify what vision of the good life we ourselves hold. Second, I noted a *normative* level of reflection that examines the adequacy of our vision of the good life. Third, I proposed a *practical* level of reflection that considers the extent to which the good life is promoted within different aspects of our pastoral encounters.

The aim of this chapter is to take us a bit further in terms of thinking about the first of these levels of reflection. Initially, we will spend some time exploring some of the difficulties associated with identifying the vision of the good life that we hold. Having done this, we will then explore some ways in which we can become more aware of our own values.

Difficulties in Identifying Our Vision of the Good Life

At first glance, the issue of how we identify the vision of the good life that influences our pastoral practice could seem very straightforward. You could sit down with a pen and a blank sheet of paper and simply write a short description of what you believe is valuable in life and what constitutes a moral approach to life. Undertaking such an exercise would not be entirely without its uses, and if you were to do this it would probably highlight a number of values and concerns that are important to you. I want to suggest here, though, that the understandings of the good life that genuinely influence our practice are not necessarily as easily identifiable as this.

There are three particular reasons that I want to discuss here as to why the values that shape our practice are not necessarily immediately obvious to us. First, following the work of Argyris and Schon (1974; see also Schon, 1991a, 1991b), I believe that it is helpful to distinguish between the 'espoused theories' that we use to explain our practice and the 'tacit knowledge' or 'theories-in-use' that actually guide what we do. Based on their research which explored practice in a range of professional and therapeutic settings, Argyris and Schon proposed the following distinction:

> When someone is asked how he [sic] would behave under certain circumstances, the answer he usually gives is his espoused theory of action for that situation. This is the theory of action to which he gives allegiance, and which, upon request, he communicates to others. However, the theory that actually governs his actions is his theory-in-use, which may or may not be compatible with his espoused theory; furthermore, the individual may or may not be aware of the incompatibility of the two theories. (1974: 6f)

Argyris and Schon's work thus raises the notion that the ideas, assumptions and values that guide our practice are not necessarily the ones that we articulate to others. It is not too difficult to think of occasions when we might consciously give an explanation to others for a particular action that does not give a full account of our motivation or thinking in that situation. The decision not fully to disclose our 'theory-in-use' in such instances may often be taken because we perceive that complete honesty on our part might be offensive to others or damaging to our own interests. In addition to such instances, however, Argyris and Schon propose that the 'theories-in-use' that actually guide our practice may also lie out of our own immediate awareness. We may therefore struggle to state our 'theories-in-use' to others, not because we are choosing not to disclose them, but because we are not fully aware of them ourselves.

Argyris and Schon's notion raises the question of why it is that our 'theories-in-use' are often implicit and out of our immediate awareness. They suggest that this is at least partly because the 'theories-in-use' that influence our practice are, in general, highly complex. It is therefore very difficult for us both to be aware of all of the nuances of the 'theory-in-use' that guides our action, at the same time as doing the action itself (see Schon 1991b: 50). For example, when we ride a bicycle it is not possible for us to be conscious of all the judgments of speed and balance that we are making at the same time as actually riding it. Similarly when we meet someone in the context of a pastoral encounter, we are not immediately aware of the assumptions that we are making about them or about the values and beliefs that influence our responses to them. The assessments that we make of real-life situations in which we find ourselves are therefore often made so rapidly that it is difficult to reconstruct the thought processes we have gone through to reach them. Indeed significant elements of our responses may well not be logical or reasoned, but non-logical or intuitive. Our 'espoused theories' may well, then, offer reasoned accounts of why we have acted in a particular way, but these do not necessarily offer a complete description of the implicit values, the assumptions and the intuitive reactions that shape our immediate responses in any given situation.

Argyris and Schon's work has considerable relevance for our discussion here. If our practice is shaped by complex beliefs and assumptions that operate so rapidly that we are barely aware of them, then it is reasonable to suggest that our practice may be influenced by values (or what Argyris and Schon call 'governing variables') that we are not necessarily conscious of. Whilst we may, as a paper exercise, be able to write down what we believe to be our general vision of the good life, this can be seen as our 'espoused theory' of the good life. This generalised statement may indeed highlight some important values and concerns that we hold, but identifying the notion of the good life that genuinely represents our 'theory-in-use' demands more detailed reflection on what we are actually doing in our specific pastoral encounters. I shall return to this point shortly.

A second reason as to why it can be difficult to establish the vision of the good life that genuinely influences our pastoral practice is that some of our values may seem so 'natural' to us that it is hard for us to recognise them as value-judgments. This situation is particularly likely to occur when we hold values that are generally shared within the wider culture or society in which we live. This point can be illustrated in the following example.

In their major study of American values, published under the title 'Habits of the Heart', Bellah et al. (1985: 3) describe four individuals who ostensibly have very different notions of the good life. Brian, a successful businessman in his early forties, has come through an experience of divorce that has left him with a much stronger sense of the importance of close marital and family relationships. Joe, a public relations director with a large company, has a strong belief in the importance of local community and puts great effort into organising community events. Margaret, a therapist in her early thirties, emphasises the importance of taking responsibility for oneself, living according to one's own values and being tolerant of others' choices. Wayne, a civil rights campaigner in his mid-thirties, sees an awareness of oppression and the struggle for justice with the oppressed as being paramount in life. On the face of it, these four people hold quite different values about what is important and good in life. Bellah and his co-authors argue, however, that at a deeper level these individuals each share a common moral assumption about the importance of individual freedom. As Bellah and his associates put it (1985: 21), each of these individuals 'assume there is something arbitrary about the goals of a good life.' Thus each of these four people share in the assumption that values are ultimately a matter of individual choice and that the good life consists in living out the values that one has chosen or found for oneself. This assumption is an expression of individualism, which Bellah and his co-authors identify as an important tradition within American culture.

The key point to be made here is that if Brian, Joe, Margaret and Wayne were to sit in a room together and debate the nature of the good life, they would probably strongly disagree with each other. This disagreement, however, would mask an underlying consensus around the American cultural value of individual freedom in deciding how to live one's life. Our notions of the good life are thus likely to involve deeply-held cultural values (for example, about the importance of the individual or of the social unit) which we are more likely to assume than be aware of, unless we encounter other cultures with radically different values to our own. The often assumed nature of these cultural values can therefore pose another complication in the process of identifying our own vision of the good life.

A third reason why identifying our visions of the good life is not a straightforward task lies in the potential for individual understandings of the good life to be contradictory or inconsistent. Argyris and Schon (1974: 20), for example, have suggested that individual's theories-in-use can lack internal consistency in both their values and assumptions. One example that they give of such inconsistency is of a group facilitator who values both a shared approach to leadership in their groups and a calm group environment. These values can, however, prove to be incompatible. For as group members become more active there is a greater potential for challenge and confrontation to develop within the group. Equally, one of the most effective ways to ensure a calm group environment is to make group members passive. The facilitator may well genuinely value both mutuality and calm interaction, but in practice may find that seeking to encourage one of these values works against the development of the other.

Argyris and Schon's example again raises the possibility that our personal vision of the good life can include values that are incompatible. At a cultural level, another example of this exists within Western individualism, in which there can be an emphasis both on the importance of individual autonomy and on the importance of finding oneself through a romantic relationship with another person (Gergen, 1991). Inconsistencies within one's vision of the good life can also be understood as an expression of life in a postmodern culture in which we are exposed to, and may have sympathy with, conflicting stories of what it means to live well (Bauman, 2000).

If we attempt to identify our personal vision of the good life using the simple kind of pen and paper exercise that we mentioned at the beginning of this part of the chapter, the likelihood is that we may fail to identify such inconsistencies and tensions in our values. If we articulate our values in a generalised way there may well be a tendency towards what, in another context, the psychoanalyst Donald Spence (1982) has referred to as 'narrative smoothing.' Our innate desire to make sense of ourselves and the world can therefore lead us to tell a story of our vision of the good life that makes sense and which fits together. Such a story may in reality, however, neglect some of the inconsistencies and tensions between the values that genuinely do shape our practice.

In summary, then, identifying our personal visions of the good life is a complex process. Generalised descriptions of our notion of the good life, based on the values that we are most conscious of, are likely to be incomplete accounts of the values that genuinely shape our practice. We have noted that this may be the case because:

1. There can be a difference between the 'espoused theories' that we use to explain our actions and the 'theories-in-use' that actually guide what we do;
2. Values that are deeply held within our particular culture are likely to seem obvious or 'natural' to us, and so we may not always be aware of these values or the degree to which they influence us;
3. Our concepts of the good life may include values that are incompatible, either in general or in specific instances. In giving a generalised overview of our particular vision of the good life, we may be likely to smooth over these inconsistencies for the sake of clarity and consistency.

Practical Ways of Identifying Our Values

We noted in the previous chapter that an awareness of the values that shape one's pastoral practice is an important element in developing a reflective approach to pastoral work. As we have seen so far in this chapter, however, identifying the vision of the good life that influences one's interactions with others is not a straightforward or easy process. How then can we attempt to identify our significant values in an adequate way?

First, in response to the complexities of identifying our 'theories-in-use', it can be suggested that we can begin to reconstruct the vision of the good life that shapes our practice through detailed reflection on specific instances of our pastoral work. By examining, in some detail, what has occurred within a particular conversation or interaction, it may be possible to identify the values that are influencing the practice of the pastoral worker. Let me give two examples of this kind of reflection.

First, in an article by McLeod and Lynch (2000) a detailed study was made of the transcript of an initial counselling session between a client, Margaret, and her person-centred counsellor, Eve. The wider purpose of this study was to examine how the stories that Margaret told about herself changed and developed during the course of her therapy. As part of this study, though, the responses that Eve made to Margaret were separated from the transcript and collated together. The kinds of responses that Eve made to what Margaret was saying to her were:

> 'so you're kind of stuck with this anger and you sort of understand it from an objective framework but inside you're just feeling really angry about this'
>
> 'and its coming out in anger?'
>
> 'and yet inside you said its really something the fear is there'
>
> 'you sound like you don't feel very good with it'
>
> 'and yet it sounded like at some point you were saying that what's really going on for you is hard for you to express?'
>
> 'a lot of feeling never really got expressed to him.'

It is evident from these responses that Eve was particularly concerned to emphasise the emotional, or affective, elements of Margaret's story. Indeed, as the first session progressed, Eve increasingly interpreted it as a story concerned with unexpressed feelings on Margaret's part: 'what's really going on for you is hard to express.' Eve's focus on the emotional dimension of Margaret's experience was further emphasised at the end of the first session, when Eve summarised her approach to their counselling relationship in the following way:

> We've made a good start. And just sort of maybe the first couple of sessions I'd like to hear sort of – the different things that are going on for you just as you're doing. And then … hopefully with time we'd be going kind of a little deeper and kind of doing it, kind of doing an emotional exploration of what's really going on for you under all this. And trying to kind of maybe – for you to be able to feel a shift in your perspective and be able to maybe see ways of changing or feeling differently about things…. It's hard to explain much more than that.

By looking at the ways in which Eve characteristically responded to Margaret in this session, it is evident that Eve believes that emotional expressiveness is an important element of healthy human functioning and that it is through such emotional expression that Margaret will be able to move to a better state of life. Associated with this valuing of emotional expression is the concept of a 'deep', 'inner' self that should find authentic expression in our lives. Eve thus tells Margaret that she hopes that they can undertake an 'exploration of what's really going on for you under all this.' From these counselling statements, it is therefore possible to identify important elements of Eve's vision of the good life as being personal authenticity and emotional self-expression. Given that Eve is a person-centred therapist it is perhaps unsurprising that her vision of the good life reflects these significant values within humanistic psychology (see, for example, Rogers, 1951, 1961, 1980). For our purposes, though, it is useful to recognise that by examining the things that a practitioner characteristically says to their client in conversation with them, it may be possible to identify some of the values that are significant for their practice.

In addition to examining what the practitioner says to their client, there can also be considerable value in reflecting on specific interactions that take place between practitioners and their clients. As an example of this, we can think about the following exchange that took place in the context of a conversation between a nurse-counsellor and a patient who was requesting an HIV test:

> Patient: Basically I'm worried that I might have AIDS. When my girlfriend, like she was on holiday in, in April with her friend … I didn't go because I was busy. She came back April … and it's now November she's just told me that this guy – this is what she told me – this guy had forced himself upon her, you know. So that's what I'm worried about.
>
> Counsellor: Mmm.
>
> Patient: And it's been unprotected sex as well.
>
> Counsellor: Right, so obviously someone had forced himself on her…. There was nothing she could do.
>
> Patient: But apparently that's what they're like out there, you know.
>
> Counsellor: (slight pause) Mmm.
>
> Patient: So that's what the score is, that's what I'm worried about. (Silverman, 1997: 25).

Towards the end of this conversational exchange, the counsellor's values are clearly, though subtly, communicated to the patient. The counsellor and patient together construct the story of how he has come to seek this test, and together they skilfully weave a narrative that preserves the moral status of both the patient and his girlfriend. The patient is therefore seen as morally responsible because he has left little time between his girlfriend's disclosure about the unprotected sex and deciding to seek an HIV test. The girlfriend is also protected from being depicted as morally irresponsible by the agreement reached by the patient and counsellor that she would not have willingly consented to unprotected sex. Having developed this story, however, the patient then makes a generalisation about the people in the country that his girlfriend visited on holiday: 'but apparently that's what they're like out there, you know'.

The fact that the counsellor pauses before responding, and when she does so responds only with a non-committal grunt, implies that she disagrees with the generalisation made by the patient, presumably because she interprets it as racist. The fact that the patient quickly moves the conversation on – 'so that's what the score is' – also suggests that he is aware of this disapproval and wants to move the conversation away from it.

This interaction is indeed a subtle one, but through a simple pause, something of the counsellor's values become evident. It would seem that, for this counsellor, an important part of the good life is an avoidance of racial or cultural prejudice, and her implied disapproval of the patient's racial generalisation reflects this value.

These two examples therefore illustrate how detailed attention to the things that a practitioner says to their client, or to the way in which they interact with that client, can help in identifying the values that shape that person's work. This kind of detailed reflection is well-established in the pastoral care movement in the United States through the practice of Clinical Pastoral Education. An integral part of CPE training programmes is the use of supervision groups in which verbatim transcripts of students' pastoral conversations with clients are studied in detail. Detailed reflection on what was said and what emerged in a particular pastoral conversation can make the pastoral carer more aware of the values and assumptions that shaped their work in this instance. The pastoral worker's guiding values can thus become clearer if attention is given to how they have responded to the client's story and what hopes or intentions they demonstrate in relation to the client's situation.

A very similar form of reflection can be identified in the use of Inter-Personal Process Recall as a method for training and supervision. In this approach developed by Kagan (1990), a practitioner will watch or listen to a recording of a conversation they have had with a client and, with the help of a facilitator, will stop the tape at each point when they can recall what they were thinking or feeling at that given moment in the conversation. The advantages of this form of reflection, as with the use of verbatim transcripts in CPE, is that pastoral workers can be helped to identify the specific thoughts, intentions and assumptions that they had at each point in a pastoral conversation. As we noted earlier, 'theories-in-use' are often so complex that we are not fully conscious of them at the same time as engaging in practice. By recollecting a pastoral conversation in detail, either through a transcript or recording, it becomes possible to 're-live' a conversation in a more reflective way and, by doing this, to reconstruct the values and beliefs that have influenced us in that particular instance. The use of transcripts or recordings in such reflection also has the advantages of avoiding the 'narrative smoothing' that often occurs if a pastoral worker simply retells the story of what happened in a particular pastoral encounter. When such a retelling occurs, the pastoral worker inevitably engages in a process of editing the pastoral conversation in order to make sense of it, and this editing can hide precisely those parts of the pastoral conversation in which the pastoral worker's values are ambiguous.

So far, we have considered how detailed attention to our practice, through examining verbatim transcripts or actual recordings of pastoral encounters, can help in identifying values that significantly influence that practice. Other methods can also be of use as we try to identify our vision of the good life. Engaging with people from other cultures, through interpersonal encounter or perhaps through reading fiction, can help to make us more aware of cultural values that are an important and often assumed part of our lives. Similarly engaging with studies that attempt to gain an overview of key trends and assumptions within our own culture can also make us more aware of some of the deeper assumptions we hold about the world (see, for example, Bellah, 1985; Taylor, 1991).

Arguably, though, one of the most useful ways of understanding more clearly the cultural values that are implicit in our own practice is to explore accounts of pastoral practice that occur in cultural contexts very different to our own or which are influenced by very different cultural assumptions. A good example of such a case study, for readers adopting a typical Western European worldview, is given by Emmanuel Lartey in his book *In Living Colour* (see Lartey, 1997: 125). This case involves Lartey's contact, as a pastoral worker, with a couple called Okai and Akousa who were at that time living in the Ghanaian city of Accra. Contrary to traditional customs, Okai and Akousa had married without the full consent of their extended families. They had one child soon after marrying (partly in an attempt to get family support for the marriage), but had not managed to have any other children in their thirteen years of marriage. This was now a significant source of tension and pain within the relationship. Okai, the husband, had come to believe that their relationship was now 'psychically' cursed, with ancestral forces attacking the marriage because of their previous disregard for the wishes of their extended families. A traditional healer that Okai had consulted suggested that they perform a traditional rite of reconciliation at the grave of Okai's dead uncle-in-law, whom he particularly believed to be a hostile ancestral presence upon the marriage. Okai was reluctant to perform this rite, however, because he felt it conflicted with his Christian convictions.

A Western pastoral practitioner looking at this case might think that one good outcome here would consist of Okai being freed from superstitious anxieties about hostile ancestral forces influencing his marriage. Another perceived good outcome from a Western viewpoint could be an emotional environment being created in which Okai and Akousa could communicate more constructively with each other and perhaps, over time, with their extended families. Lartey's pastoral practice in this case, however, sought to take seriously the traditional African cultural world-view which places great emphasis on the importance of the relationship with the extended family, both the living and the dead. Part of his practice in this case was indeed to help Okai and Akousa communicate more of their thoughts and feelings to each other. Another important element, however, was that of Okai and Akousa visiting the grave of his dead uncle-in-law to express both their feelings of anger and frustration, and their desire for forgiveness and reconciliation. This, in turn, led them to meet with their living extended families to attempt some process of reconciliation with them as well. In its sensitivity to the importance and integrity of traditional African culture, Lartey's practice here thus sought to move Okai and Akousa closer towards a view of the good life which included an emphasis on the importance of good relations with one's extended family, both the living and the dead. This notion of the good life contrasts with contemporary Western views in which the extended family is often not seen as central to our well-being and in which the notion of our relationship with the dead is very rarely given any importance. Through exploring case studies such as this, then, we may become more conscious of the cultural assumptions (and notions of the good life) that influence our pastoral work with others.

Another approach by which we may begin to gain a better understanding of the complex values that we hold may be to think in terms of 'stories of the good life' that are significant for us. A 'story of the good life' can be understood as a particular narrative that expresses for us something of what it means to live well. One of the features of narrative is that it can hold contrasting values and ideas together in the same story in a way that it is much harder to do if we are thinking in abstract, propositional terms. For example, in the TV programme *Ally McBeal* the central characters (particularly Ally herself) are frequently caught between the desire to find fulfillment through a romantic relationship with another person (and the accompanying wish to avoid loneliness) and the contrasting desire to live as an autonomous, competent adult. Often within the plot-line, as one of the characters moves towards one of these versions of the good life, they find themselves aware that they are moving away from the other. Thus, as Ally develops a close relationship with another person she often becomes increasingly aware that she is becoming dependent on another person and losing her autonomy. Equally, when she is single, she has a strong desire to find a partner and values her personal autonomy to a lesser degree. Narratives are able to capture and express such tensions and contradictions in our values with much greater sophistication than if we attempt to express our vision of the good life in terms of an abstract list of values. By attending to stories that we tell about our own lives, or by attending to other stories within our culture that are meaningful to us, it may therefore be possible to become aware of complexities within our values than if we simply think about visions of the good life in more abstract terms.

In response to the three difficulties that we identified earlier in describing our vision of the good life, three possible responses can be suggested:

1. We may become more aware of the values that guide our practice if we reflect in detail on specific instances of our pastoral conversations. Such reflection is likely to be more valuable if we work with transcripts or recordings of these conversations, rather than with our own narrative re-tellings of them.
2. We may become more aware of values that are deeply-held within our own cultures by engaging in some way with other cultures (in particular, accounts of pastoral practice in other cultures) or with studies of values within our particular culture.
3. We may be more able to identify complexities and tensions within our values if we think in terms of stories of the good life that are significant to us, rather than working simply with abstract notions of what it means to live well.

Clearly to pursue these proposals involves a serious commitment to reflecting on one's own values. Many pastoral workers might object that they do not have the time or other resources to enable them to engage in the kind of reflection that we have briefly discussed here. For hard-pressed pastoral workers this may indeed be the case, and questions are certainly raised by these proposals about the commitment to the ongoing supervision of practice within religious institutions and organisations. Despite these practical difficulties, there is still value in recognising the complexities involved in identifying our personal visions of the good life, if only to discourage us from developing superficial notions of the values that guide our practice.

Summary

In this chapter we have considered some of the issues involved with identifying the vision of the good life that informs our practice. It has become clear that a serious attempt to identify our vision of the good life will not be easy and faces some significant difficulties. These difficulties are not insurmountable, however, and becoming more aware of our significant values is possible if we have sufficient resources and motivation to think in detail about our practice and what assumptions we hold about the world. This chapter has focused on the concrete issue of the nature of the values that genuinely influence our practice. Thinking rigorously about the good life in relation to pastoral practice will involve not only identifying our own values, but also asking more general questions about how we can achieve a satisfactory idea of what the good life actually is. These more general questions will be the focus of the next chapter.

3

Pursuing a vision of the good life

Within the academic literature on pastoral care and counselling, various definitions have been offered in recent years of the appropriate aims and nature of pastoral practice. Clebsch and Jaekle's (1967: 4) often-cited definition proposes that pastoral care 'consists of helping acts, done by representative Christian persons, directed towards the healing, sustaining, guiding and reconciling of troubled persons whose troubles arise in the context of ultimate meanings and concerns.' Howard Clinebell (1984) has proposed that pastoral care and counselling 'involve the utilisation by persons in ministry of one-to-one or small group relationships to enable healing, empowerment and growth to take place in individuals and their relationships.' Emmanuel Lartey (1997) suggests that pastoral care 'seeks to foster people's growth as full human beings together with the development of ecologically holistic communities in which all persons may live humane lives.'

Whilst such definitions serve a useful function as signposts to what is important in pastoral practice, they each beg a common set of questions. These questions concern what is meant by terms such as 'healing' and 'growth'. What are the characteristics of a healthy life, for example? How do we know if someone is 'growing' in ways that are genuinely positive and constructive? What does it mean for a person to live a 'full' or 'proper' human existence? From our discussion in Chapter 1, we can recognise that these are fundamentally questions about the nature of the good life: what does it mean to live well and to live morally? Theoretical discussions of the nature and aims of pastoral practice therefore lead, sooner or later, to questions about how we should define the good life that pastoral practice seeks to move people towards.

If we have spent time reflecting on the values that shape our own pastoral practice (as was discussed in the previous chapter), then we are led to a similar set of questions. If I come to realise that I have a particular understanding of the good life that influences my practice with others, then this begs the question as to whether my vision of the good life is adequate. Does it give a proper account of what is Good and True within our existence?

Theoretical discussions of the nature of pastoral care, and practical reflection on our own personal values, can therefore lead us to ask more general questions about how we can best define the good life. The aim of this chapter is to consider some fundamental issues about the pursuit of such a definition. Some readers might find the material in this chapter a bit too theoretical for their liking. If this is so, you may wish, for the time being, to skip to the following chapters that explore different dimensions of the pastoral relationship. If you do skip this chapter for now, you will find it helpful to return to it later on as reflection on specific examples of pastoral practice does eventually lead to the more general issues that are explored here.

Within this chapter we will first look at a framework of questions and resources that can help us to think about the nature of the good life. We will then think about whether it is possible or desirable to seek a single, universal definition of what it means to live well and to live morally. Finally, I will suggest two ideas that I believe to be important elements of any adequate definition of the good life and which may give us some indication of what the nature of constructive visions of the good life for pastoral practice might be.

A Framework for Thinking about the Nature of the Good Life

Arguably the most important writer on the subject of moral reflection in relation to pastoral practice in recent years has been the American pastoral theologian, Don Browning. Through his writing since the mid-1970s, Browning has highlighted the moral assumptions within secular and pastoral therapeutic practice (see Browning, 1976; 1987; 1988), and has proposed a specific model for moral reflection in relation to pastoral practice (see Browning, 1983). This work has also led Browning to develop a sophisticated account of how practical theology should be conducted, which gives a primary emphasis to the importance of developing practical moral wisdom (Browning, 1991). It is not possible to do full justice to the complexity of Browning's work here, but for our purposes now it will be helpful to focus on two key points that he has made that are relevant to our enquiry about how to pursue a vision of the good life.

The first point to be made about Browning's work concerns his idea about different levels of moral reflection. As we engage in the process of thinking critically about the nature of the good life, Browning (1983: 53–71) identifies four different levels of reflection that we can usefully engage in[1]. The first of these levels is what Browning describes as the *metaphorical* level of reflection. The primary concern at this level is with thinking about what basic metaphors or concepts we use to understand existence. Do we understand the world to be a place in which God, in some sense, is present and what is the nature of this divine presence? What is the fundamental nature of life and death? Do we, as individuals, face the prospect of an eternal existence after death or are we reincarnated through a series of different lives? This level of reflection therefore explores our basic assumptions about the nature of reality. Thinking critically at this metaphorical level of reflection involves not only identifying the basic beliefs we hold about existence, however. Rather, it also involves a critical questioning of what effects these beliefs have on the way in which we perceive and relate to individuals and wider social structures.

Focusing on these questions is important for our enquiry about the nature of the good life, because our understanding of what it means to live well and to live morally is ultimately inseparable from our basic assumptions about the nature of life. Thus, for example, the Buddhist notion of the good life is that of nirvana, in which it is possible to experience final release from the cycle of rebirth. This aspiration makes sense, however, only in the context of a wider belief system in which life is seen as characterised by suffering (*dukka*) and an ongoing cycle of reincarnation in which one is reborn into new existences in which suffering may be experienced (Keown, 2000).

The second level that Browning identifies is the *obligational* level of reflection. This level of thinking is concerned with identifying any general moral principles that should characterise a moral approach to existence. Examples of these would be the notion of loving one's neighbour as oneself or of never treating another person as a means to an end. Reflection about the nature of the good life at this second level would thus attempt to identify basic elements of what it means to live morally.

The third level of reflection described by Browning is the *tendency-need* level. The focus here is on what constitute central human qualities and needs. Are there certain aspects of human existence which require satisfaction if a person is to live a full life? If so, what are these different needs (for example, the need for emotional authenticity, for spiritual development, for relationships, for sexual expression, etc.)? Furthermore, how can we distinguish between these different needs? Are some more important or more basic than others, and does every one of them require satisfaction if a person is to live a full life? At this third level of reflection, then, the fundamental issue is how we can define the central elements of what is needed to live a full human life.

The fourth level of reflection is what Browning refers to as the *contextual-predictive* level. For our purposes here, this level involves thinking about what the nature of the good life is in the particular culture and historical context in which we find ourselves. Such reflection thus raises the important question about whether the good life can be given a universal definition that holds true for all times and places, or whether the nature of what it means to live well may actually be different in different contexts.

The framework that Don Browning has proposed for moral reflection in relation to pastoral practice therefore highlights certain levels of questions that may guide our pursuit of an understanding of the good life. In summary these are:

- The 'metaphorical' level: what basic assumptions should we make about reality that will provide a wider context in which an adequate concept of the good life will make sense?
- The 'obligational' level: what constitute the basic elements of living a moral life?
- The 'tendency-need' level: what are the fundamental elements of what it means to live a full human life? Do any of these 'needs' have greater priority or importance than others?
- The 'contextual-predictive' level: what does it mean to live the good life in the particular historical and cultural context in which I find myself?

The second observation to be made about Browning's work concerns his ideas about what the key resources are that can begin to help us answer these different levels of questions. The first resource that Browning notes in relation to such moral reflection is that of our *experience*. He observes that our experience is significant for our moral thinking initially as a source of motivation to engage in such reflection. Questions about how we should act in particular circumstances, or more general questions about what it means to live well, may be interesting as purely theoretical or conceptual issues. These questions arise most significantly for us, however, when we ourselves experience uncertainty about how we should act or what kind of life we should aspire to lead. Thus, when we ourselves struggle to understand how we can best conduct our relationships, express our sexuality or prioritise different claims on our lives, we are drawn to moral reflection in a more profound and raw way than when we treat these questions as a purely academic exercise.

As other pastoral theologians have emphasised, our experience is important not only as a source of motivation for moral thinking but also as a point where our more theoretical discussions must be grounded (see, for example, Lartey, 2000; Pattison, 2000b). Thus, as we think in more abstract terms about the nature of the good life, our own stories and experiences become an important touchstone against which we can assess the viability or usefulness of more abstract ideas that we develop. Any notion of the good life that we develop which fails to incorporate our own lived experience of what it means to live well will be hollow and inadequate. Within this category of experience, it is helpful not only to include our own experiences, but to pay attention to what the stories and experiences of others may have to tell us about the nature of the good life as well. Indeed, attending to the experiences of those who are marginalised within our culture may enable us to gain a much fuller and more complex notion of the good life than if we attend simply to experiences that seem more familiar or mainstream.

The second resource that Browning regards as important for moral reflection could broadly be described as *reason*. This resource includes both our general capacity for critical and rational reflection about the nature of the good life and particular theoretical models (whether, for example, philosophical, political, sociological or psychological) which attempt to give some definition to what it means to live well and to live morally. In attempting to answer questions about what general ethical principles are important for the moral life, or about how we might define central human needs, such rational resources can play an important role. Critical thinking will enable us to evaluate ideas and assess their strengths, weaknesses and implications. Furthermore, thinking critically about particular abstract theories, for example, Aristotle's idea of the good life as the use of reason in the pursuit of virtue (see Arrington, 1999), or Carl Rogers' (1961) notion of the good life as close awareness of one's moment-to-moment experience, we can further clarify for ourselves what we believe to be central elements of what it means to live well.

The third important resource within Browning's model for practical moral reflection can again be broadly categorised under the heading *revelation*. What we have said so far in this chapter about ways of enquiring about the nature of the good life could potentially be used by anyone regardless of whether or not they have any religious affiliations or commitments. In pursuing a vision of the good life, however, pastoral workers will generally want their thinking to be informed by the particular religious tradition to which they are committed. To describe revelation as a resource for moral reflection in relation to pastoral practice is therefore to recognise the importance of the symbols, stories, doctrines, experiences and practices of particular religious communities in the pursuit of such a vision. Thus, for example, Browning himself proposes that, at the 'metaphorical' level of Christian moral reflection, the images of 'God as Creator' and 'God as Redeemer-Judge' should help to provide an understanding of the fundamental nature of existence within which any concept of the good life or of specific moral action should make sense. Reflection at the other levels that

Browning identifies can clearly also be informed by religious ideas about the moral life and the nature of the human condition.

The relative weight to which we give to experience, reason and revelation in our moral thinking is a contentious issue. Those pastoral workers who associate with conservative elements of their particular religious tradition are likely to want to give primary emphasis to *revelation* in their thinking. Those whose sympathies lie more with traditional liberal theology are more likely to emphasise *reason*, whereas many writers associated with contemporary developments in practical theology will wish to ensure that *experience* is given due regard in such reflection. The different degrees of authority that can be attributed to experience, reason and revelation, together with the different ways in which these resources might individually be interpreted and used in moral reflection, point to the complex array of pathways that can be taken, as one pursues a vision of the good life. This suggests, as is indeed the case, that the definition of the good life in pastoral contexts can be heavily contested and that the different experiences, theoretical perspectives and religious commitments of pastoral workers can lead to very contrasting ideas about what constitute good ends or aims for pastoral practice.

Summarising what we have said so far about Browning's work, it is clear that pursuing a vision of the good life for pastoral practice is a complex process that can involve both honest reflection on our own experience and critical, inter-disciplinary, thinking. Browning sees this process as one that begins with our experience, one that critically compares insights from relevant secular and religious sources, and one which involves reflection at a number of different levels of questioning. Whilst the framework that I have described here sets some broad parameters for the pursuit of a vision of the good life, it is clear that it offers little more than the bare bones of what such critical reflection entails. If you wish to look at texts that will help you to think about these issues in much more detail, then some suggestions of useful resources are given in the 'Further Reading' section towards the end of the book.

A Universal Vision of the Good Life?

So far in this chapter we have given some thought to what is involved in pursuing a vision of the good life. One question that is raised by this moral exploration, though, is what we hope to find at the end of our quest. Do we expect to be able to achieve a single definition of the good life that will be valid for all people at all times and places? Is such a goal possible, or indeed desirable?

The issue of whether a single universal definition of the good life is possible is again a contested one. Key figures within the history of moral philosophy such as Aristotle and Thomas Aquinas have sought to define the true and objective essence of a good life, and the notion that a final understanding of the good life can be reached through rational reflection remains amongst some moral philosophers today. On the face of it, the idea that we can reach some final definition of the essence of what it means to live well and to live morally has some validity. After all, unless like Jean-Paul Sartre (1973), we believe that there are no ultimate values, it would appear to make sense to say that with sufficient effort and wisdom we could reach a final understanding of the true nature of the good life. A significant problem arises, though, as to how we can objectively demonstrate whether a particular view of the good life is true or not. The philosopher Richard Rorty describes his growing awareness of this problem in the following way:

> The more philosophers I read, the clearer it seemed that each of them could carry their views back to first principles which were incompatible with the first principles of their opponents, and that none of them ever got to that fabled place 'beyond hypotheses'. There seemed to be nothing like a neutral standpoint from which these alternative first principles could be evaluated. But if there were no such standpoint, then the whole idea of 'rational certainty', and the whole … idea of replacing passion by reason, seemed not to make much sense. (Rorty, 1999: 10)

In other words, when different philosophical views of the world are compared together, it becomes clear that each rests on a certain set of assumptions about the world. Yet, Rorty claims, there appears to be no objective or authoritative way of judging which assumptions are better or more true than others. There might indeed be certain views of the world that we find more constructive and appealing than others, but this would seem to be more a case of our personal preferences and cultural background rather than anything more objective. Rorty's observation, then, calls into question whether we can reach a view of the good life that we can prove to be the definitive and final account.

Even if, we acknowledge that we might not be able to prove that any one definition of the good life is better than any other, we might still feel that a particular view of what it means to live well is important and demands our commitment. In this case we may feel that we must claim that this view is universally valid, even if we cannot objectively prove that this is the case. To support this definition of the good life we might try to argue that it is upheld by sources that go beyond reason, such as God's influence on our inner conscience or through the words of Holy Scriptures. It seems possible, then, for us to assert particular ideas about the good life as being universally true, regardless of whether we can prove this to be the case to everyone's satisfaction. But the question remains as to how desirable or feasible this approach actually is.

One difficulty concerns the complexities involved in trying to distil a single definitive vision of the good life from a particular religious tradition or set of texts. Pastoral theologians and theological ethicists have indeed claimed that a single, normative vision of the good life can be found within the text of the Bible. Even if these claims are tempered by the acknowledgement that discerning this vision is a complex task and one that requires constant re-working as our own cultural situation changes (see, for example, Gerkin, 1991), there are still difficulties with this view. The Hebrew Scriptures and Christian Bible are, for example, largely narrative based and it is notoriously difficult to establish one clear, single meaning from a collection of stories. Different scriptural stories contain different emphases (for example, compare the emphases of the two stories of creation in Genesis 1 and Genesis 2), and this raises the question of which stories we choose to value over other stories. Furthermore, even within a single narrative, we are left with the question of whose perspective we read the story from. In the story of Hagar being sent away by Abraham, do we read the story from Abraham's perspective or Hagar's? Similarly in the story of Solomon's construction of the Temple in Jerusalem, do we read this story from the perspective of Solomon or from the perspective of those who were conscripted into forced labour for this project? The question of whom we choose to sympathise with in the narrative has important consequences for whether we think the actions reported in the story are an expression of a good approach to life or not (see, for example, Brueggeman, 1993).

To claim, then, that a narrative-based collection of scriptural texts can easily yield a clear, single vision of the good life thus ignores the complexity of the range of moral ideas evident within these texts. Again we find that, whilst we might claim a particular view of the good life is ultimately true on theological grounds, this vision may reflect more our own prior convictions and preferences than some pure religious resource.

Another problem with clear, universal definitions of the good life concerns their potentially oppressive nature. I recently went to an exhibition of contemporary British art, and was struck by one exhibit that was a series of paintings depicting a vision of what an ideal world might be like. These paintings were simple, but graphic, images of ideas that were printed at the bottom of each picture. Some examples of these ideas were 'Money is destroyed', 'Land is shared', 'People leave the armed forces' and 'Hurts are healed'. Initially I felt attracted by these images, but then felt a growing sense of unease. Two other paintings focused on the ideas 'Roads are dug up' and 'People build their own houses and grow their own food'. As I looked at these two pictures I became aware of how the ideal vision that the paintings represented was not one that I really shared. This vision was ultimately one of a return to nature, which emphasised the value of simple, self-sufficient living off the land. As someone who lives in a city, and who enjoys its social and cultural opportunities, this ideal of a life living off the land seemed constraining and, to be honest, dull. I was also conscious of how the aspirations depicted in these paintings could also serve vested interests. The notion of a shared land in which people can live on small, self-sufficient holdings has, for example, recently been used in Zimbabwe by Robert Mugabe, partly to shore up his political support amongst certain sections of the community and to weaken the economic and political base of potential opponents.

This illustration about these paintings points to the potential for clear definitions of a good life or good society to function in *hegemonic* ways. 'Hegemony' was a concept developed by the Italian political and cultural theorist, Antonio Gramsci. Gramsci (1996) argued that ideas are hegemonic when they exclude or annihilate other ways of thinking about reality and when they serve to uphold the existing social order. Hegemony is therefore a state in which a set of ideas is uncritically supported within a particular social group and in which these ideas help vested interests within that group. It is possible to see how ideas about the good life can become hegemonic in pastoral settings. For example, in many Christian churches there is a presumption that the appropriate form of expression for human sexuality is ultimately heterosexual marriage. Whilst this idea can find explicit expression, for example in sermons or books produced within those churches, it also functions in implicit ways through the kinds of activities that these churches choose to engage in and by the kind of people who are made to feel welcome or unwelcome in these groups. In this instance, this understanding of sexuality can be understood as functioning in a hegemonic way. First, as an assumption about the nature of appropriate sexual expression it can exclude other perspectives (for example gay and lesbian experiences) and does not allow these a proper space to be expressed. The effective silencing of other voices means that it is harder for the assumption that heterosexual marriage is the ideal to be challenged and thought about in a more critical way (see Stuart, 1995). Second, though, this view of sexuality can also serve a hegemonic function in these churches by preserving the status and power within those churches of people who are themselves in heterosexual marriages. Thus whilst lip service may be paid within many churches to the validity of a celibate, gay lifestyle, in practice it is very difficult to think of many people who hold power and status within the church who are openly celibate and gay.

The concept of hegemony can help us to be more aware that the issue of defining the good life is not simply an abstract or esoteric quest. Rather, attempts to define the good life take place in real human communities and societies. The ways in which we construct these definitions have the power to help or hurt people, to include different experiences or to exclude all but a select few, and to support uncritically, existing social structures and vested interests or to open these up to more honest and open critical scrutiny. To go back to our earlier question, then, the search for a clear and universal vision of the good life can, in some important respects, have dangerous elements to it. If we seek to assert a clear idea of what it means to live well on others then there is a danger that we will be silencing other perspectives and experiences that are equally as valid as our own. Similarly, there is a danger that such clear definitions can function in ways that uphold existing social arrangements and restrict the potential for raising more critical questions about social justice and human well-being.

In this chapter, then, we have seen that the search for a universal definition of the good life is problematic. There is, first, the issue of how we can ever prove to everyone's satisfaction that a particular notion of what it means to live well is genuinely correct. Second, there is the problem that, even if we choose to assert a particular view of the good life, perhaps on the basis of some divinely sanctioned authority, this definition of the good life may actually be unhelpfully exclusive and damaging to other people.

Where does this leave us in our quest to gain a better understanding of the good life? One option is that we could abandon the search for a single definition of the good life and propose that everyone's notion of it, whatever form it takes, is equally valid. This approach seems unlikely to promote human well-being, though, precisely because it allows for understandings of the good life to be developed that are damaging to other people. The idea of the good life that may be held by a serial sexual abuser of children or by a white supremacist contains elements that, if enacted, are highly detrimental to other people. If we say that all notions of the good life are valid, then we leave ourselves in a position where we cannot criticise views that we recognise as deeply unhealthy. In this book I want to suggest that there may be a useful middle way between a simplistic search for universal definitions of the good life and between the abandonment of this quest as unworkable. The middle way that I propose is one in which we seek a vision of the good life, but in which we recognise that our current understanding of it is always provisional and subject to change as we are exposed to new experiences and viewpoints. In pursuing this middle way, I also want to suggest that there are certain markers that are an important part of an adequate definition of the good life and that, whilst valid visions of the good life may differ in their detail, these markers should occupy at least some part of any valid definition. In the final part of this chapter I will examine briefly what these markers are and, through doing this, begin to think about what may be important elements of a vision of the good life that can support constructive pastoral practice.

The Role of the 'Other' and Personal Authenticity in the Good Life

Over recent years a number of writers working at both a popular and academic level have raised a related set of concerns about the condition of contemporary Western culture. These concerns are focused around the idea that our society is increasingly characterised by self-absorption, narcissism, anxiety about one's standing with others and a primary desire for self-fulfilment. Whilst writers such as Christopher Lasch (1984) and Richard Sennett (1986) have attempted to give sophisticated explanations of the social processes that lie behind this trend, this line of thinking is demonstrated in a more straightforward way in the writing of the American psychologist, Paul Vitz. Vitz (1994) claimed that humanistic psychology, which has been influential in North America, reflects a central doctrine of 'selfism' in which the pursuit of self-actualisation is seen as a greater good than any other commitment or moral standard. Whilst Vitz's analysis of that movement was arguably too simplistic, his phrase 'selfism' does express an ongoing anxiety held by some within our culture that we are becoming more absorbed with our own desires and aspirations than with our responsibilities to others and to wider society.

In the context of this concern with 'selfism', it is perhaps unsurprising that one of the twentieth-century philosophers whose work is increasingly in vogue is Emmanuel Levinas[2]. Central to Levinas' thought is the notion of the fundamental significance of the 'Other', and I wish to suggest here that his thought highlights one crucial element of any satisfactory definition of the good life.

Fundamental to Levinas' thought has been his idea that our existence is primarily an ethical one (see Peperzak, 1995, 1996; Davis, 1996). He has criticised the main preoccupation within Western philosophy to attempt to develop objective and comprehensive explanations of the nature of reality. Rather Levinas has proposed that our lives are fundamentally given meaning by that which transcends our capacity for rational explanation, for which he uses the term the 'Other.' For Levinas, the basic fact of our existence is that we are responsible for the 'Other'; this is, as he puts it, 'an obligation which is … prior to every engagement (Peperzak, 1996: 81).' At its simplest, then, Levinas is saying that before we attempt any thought or action, we are always confronted with the prior claim that the 'Other' places on us for our care and respect. Whilst the 'Other' is always that which transcends me and my capacity for understanding, in concrete terms I engage with the 'Other' through others (specific people) that I encounter. It is thus through my relations with others that I can therefore live out my responsibility to respect and care for that which is beyond me, the 'Other'.

At this point, you may be feeling that Levinas is really just using complex language to convey the simple point that we should live our lives with due regard to other people. To think this, though, would be to miss the radical nature of what Levinas is saying. Rather than saying that concern for other people is simply an important ethical principle, Levinas is claiming that it is our responsibility for the 'Other' that determines the nature of our existence before anything else. Writing about the claim that the 'Other' places on us, Levinas, for example, comments that 'instead of offending my freedom it calls it to responsibility and founds it' (Davis, 1996: 49). Thus everything about myself, my freedom, my capacity to think and feel, my ability to act, is given shape and meaning by my responsibility to that which is beyond me. My responsibility to respect and care for the 'Other' is the fact that precedes all other facts about my existence and which stretches out inexhaustibly ahead of me.

If an unhealthy preoccupation with the status and development of the self is a genuine risk in our culture, then Levinas' thought seems a radically alternative way in which we might conceive of our existence and what it means to live well. Levinas' emphasis on the significance of the 'Other' points to a life of radical service to that which is beyond ourselves, which finds expression through our particular relationships with other people.

I would want to suggest here that Levinas' ideas highlight one strand that is an essential element of any adequate definition of the good life. Colin Davis (1996: 48) captures this element well when he comments that 'the Other makes me realise that I share the world, that it is not my unique possession'. An adequate definition of the good life must therefore acknowledge that my desires and aspirations are not necessarily the most important thing to which I should be committed, and that I live in a shared world in which care and respect for the 'Other' has a fundamental claim upon me.

Part of the value of Levinas' thought is the degree of emphasis that he places on the significance of the 'Other', which helps us to recognise the fundamental nature of this moral claim on us. At the same time, the strength of Levinas' emphasis on the 'Other' also contains significant dangers. With the growing literature on shame, for example, there is a recognition that if a person finds meaning and value only through the service of others then this can be a reflection of a psychological deficit on their part, in which their own 'self' is so fragile that it can only find value through emotional merger with others (Pattison, 2000a). Similarly, as a number of writers have observed, the notion of negating oneself in the service of others has at times served an ideological function in encouraging people in subservient positions not to question their lot and to see their acquiescence to others' vested interests as a moral virtue. Thus, whilst we might agree with Levinas' emphasis on the

'Other', it is also important to acknowledge the value of appropriate self-regard. This can lead us to balance an ethic of valuing the 'Other', with an ethic of personal authenticity.

The idea of personal authenticity as morally important is one that emerges in Western culture from the work of Jean-Jacques Rousseau, and finds its clearest development in his novel, *The New Heloise* (see Ferrara, 1993). Two of the central characters in this novel are Julie, the only daughter of an aristocrat who hopes to improve their family's poor fortunes through her marriage, and Saint-Preux, a kind man who is in love with Julie but who has no social standing. A focal point of the narrative within this novel is a decision that Julie has to face between developing a relationship with Saint-Preux and between marrying a man that she does not love in a socially useful match arranged by her father. Ultimately Julie decides to end her relationship with Saint-Preux and to marry the other man, and the remainder of the novel concerns the outworking of this decision.

What is significant about this novel is that Rousseau introduces the original idea that standards of morality that we would normally see as important can be called into question by motivations or feelings that seem integral to our sense of personal identity. One of the characters in the novel tries to persuade Julie to pursue her relationship with Saint-Preux, by saying 'You shall never efface love's strong impression without at the same time effacing all the exquisite sentiments which you have received from nature (see Ferrara, 1993: 96).' He continues, 'When you'll have no more love left, nothing worth esteem will remain in you either.' Thus Julie, who is committed to the moral principle of not causing her father to be unhappy, is here being confronted with the idea that to fail to act in accordance with her feelings of love would diminish her own personal being. The demands of conventional morality are seen here as subject to suspension when they contradict our own deep sense of who we are.

This ethic of authenticity would seem to run the risk, of degenerating into the kind of preoccupation with self-fulfilment above all else that would run entirely counter to a regard for the 'Other'. The kind of ethic of authenticity arising out of Rousseau's work need not deteriorate into this kind of amoral self-obsession, however. An important distinction needs to be made here between acting on the basis of any feelings or desires that one has regardless of any other moral issues involved, and acting on those feelings and desires that are a fundamental part of who one is. The former approach is indeed a form of self-obsession that is detrimental to a moral life. As such, it demonstrates a disinterest towards wider moral questions. The latter approach, acknowledges that, in some instances, it is more important to be authentic than to follow conventional morality. This need not involve a disregard for moral issues, and is more likely to involve a painful awareness of the tragic nature of the conflict between duty and profound feeling.

I would want to argue here, then, that an ethic of personal authenticity provides an important counter-balance to Levinas' emphasis on the significance of the 'Other'. Without a proper regard for one's own personal being, a commitment to the 'Other' risks becoming a replacement for appropriate self-esteem or a damaging approach to relationships in which it is oneself that is exploited. Similarly, an emphasis on authenticity which lacks a recognition of the importance of the 'Other' can become an unhealthy means of self-assertion to the consistent detriment of others. I would propose that an understanding of both the significance of the 'Other' and of the value of personal authenticity is essential to an adequate view of the good life.

These two notions, of proper regard for other and for self, represent two poles between which a range of more specific ideas of the good life can be developed. Whilst we may not always experience a tension between the value of self and other, it is almost inevitable that we will encounter some situations in which we are forced to choose between the interests of ourselves and others. In such cases we may be forced to choose between our own profound feelings and the claims that others have upon us. This will inevitably involve one of these two poles of the good life collapsing into the other, and whenever this occurs, whatever the outcome, we are unlikely to be able to avoid a sense of tragedy.

So what might this mean for pastoral practice? A central part of this book's argument so far has been that pastoral practice is always informed by the particular notion of the good life held by the pastoral worker. If it is true that an adequate vision of the good life should include both a commitment to the 'Other' and a regard for personal authenticity, then what implications might this have for how we think about pastoral practice?

The detailed exploration of this question in relation to different aspects of the pastoral relationship will be the focus of the following four chapters of this book. For the time being, though, the following key ideas can be identified.

First, if a pastoral worker has a notion of the good life that emphasises these values, then they will have a particular understanding of what constitute desirable *aims* of their pastoral practice. If we understand the good life as involving both a commitment to the 'Other' and a valuing of personal authenticity, then our pastoral practice will seek to help people to live within the parameters of these two values. If a client shows fundamental disregard for themselves or others, then this will be a concern for a pastoral worker operating with those values. In a more positive sense, pastoral practice could be understood as a process of enabling people to encounter both their core selves and others in deeper and more constructive ways. For many pastoral workers, helping to deepen someone's awareness of the 'Other' will also have the sense of enabling people to deepen their experience of ultimate transcendence, or God.

The pastoral worker is also likely to have to support clients as they struggle between the demands of these two poles of the good life. For example, in situations where a client may be thinking about pursuing a divorce or terminating a pregnancy, the client may face some extremely difficult choices between the expression of who they are and their responsibility towards others. Recognising the importance, both of the significance of the 'Other' and of the importance of personal authenticity, will mean that the pastoral worker will have no straightforward answers as their client engages in this struggle. Rather the pastoral worker may find themselves sharing in the pain and uncertainty of the tragic dilemma.

Second, valuing personal authenticity and the significance of the 'Other' will also lead pastoral workers to think in particular ways about the *process* of the pastoral practice that they engage in. For example, a commitment to care for and respect the 'Other' means approaching pastoral work not only with a concern for others' well-being, but with the recognition of the 'Otherness' of those that we encounter. This means acknowledging that we cannot collapse people that we encounter into preformed ideas of what is wrong in their lives and what it would mean for them to experience well-being. Rather each encounter with another person becomes a challenge to encounter their 'Otherness' and to be open to where they may transcend our existing ideas of who they are, who we are, or what life may be like.

Similarly, a regard for personal authenticity means that we cannot neglect our own presence in the pastoral relationship. Our commitment to others' well-being should not, then, lead us to lose a proper sense of who we are in that relationship or to us being exploited by others. This acknowledgement of the importance of the pastoral worker's own authenticity can also raise complex issues when clients choose actions that profoundly contradict the values that the pastoral worker them-selves deeply hold.

Summary

In this chapter we have thought about some of the resources, processes and problems that may be involved in attempting to define the good life. In exploring the ideas of the 'Other' and personal authenticity, we have also considered two elements that I would suggest are important elements of any definition of what it means to live well. Thinking about the nature of the good life in these theoretical terms is important in helping us to develop a reflective approach to our lives and our practice, but there are further important questions that need to be asked about the good life and pastoral work. For even if the pastoral worker has a clear vision of the good life that inspires and underpins their practice, what is it in real pastoral encounters that can help or hinder people's experience of this good life? In the following chapters, we will turn our attention to four different dimensions of the pastoral encounter and ask what, in each of these dimensions, can help or hinder human well-being?

Notes

1 In his model of moral reflection for pastoral practice, Browning actually identifies five different levels for reflection. We shall not consider the fifth of these here, however. This fifth level, which Browning refers to as the 'rule-role' level, is concerned with questions about how we should act in a particular situation and thus has a more specific focus than enquiring about the nature of the good life more generally. Browning's other four levels of moral reflection have a more general focus and are therefore more relevant to broader questions about what it means to live well and to live morally.

2 Levinas' work is drawing interest at this moment in time, not only because of his robust advocacy of the significance of the 'Other', but also because his attempt to build an ethic on a non-rational basis is attractive to a postmodern culture.

4

The social context of the pastoral encounter

So far, then, we have noted the importance of the pastoral worker's vision of the good life for their practice, and thought both about how we might identify our own core values and how we might reflect on what the nature of the good life is. In the remaining chapters of this book we will now turn our attention to more specific questions of pastoral practice. In any given pastoral encounter, what can actually promote or hinder a person's experience of the good life? What are the different aspects of the pastoral relationship that have a bearing on whether that relationship promotes well-being or not?

The way in which we will begin to explore these questions is to think about the significance of the context of the pastoral relationship. In what ways can the context in which the pastoral relationship takes place have an effect on people's ability to experience the good life? This question is an important subject for reflection. An increasing number of writers have observed that, at least partly under the influence of psychotherapeutic concepts, modern theories of pastoral care have tended to focus on the care of the individual and to neglect the wider social context of the individual's suffering (for example, Selby, 1983; Leech, 1994). To ignore the social context of human suffering, however, runs the risk of failing to address some of the most significant causes of that distress. In his book on *Pastoral Care and Liberation Theology*, Stephen Pattison makes the following observation:

> Pastoral care has fallen into the trap of thinking too narrowly about how people's welfare might be sought and their potential developed. In doing so, it may actually inadvertently work against its intentions to promote well-being; it may also collude with some of the social and political forces which create and maintain human suffering…. As we have seen in the analysis of the situation of mentally ill people … the locus of suffering may be the individual, but some of the factors that cause the individual to suffer lie far beyond any individual's control or influence. Poverty and unemployment, for example, are essentially social problems which have severe consequences for individuals, but actually require social and political solutions. If such solutions are excluded by those who claim to seek the welfare of individuals, then present suffering is perpetuated and a replication of such suffering for other people will be inevitable in the future. (Pattison, 1994: 208, 214)

If we are concerned to promote the good life through pastoral practice, it therefore follows that we should be concerned with the extent to which the cultural practices and social structures, within which we work, also help or hinder human well-being. Bringing a moral perspective to bear on pastoral practice thus involves more than thinking about the professional basis of the pastoral relationship or the content of particular pastoral conversations. Pastoral practice, informed by a vision of the good life, should inevitably involve critical reflection on the social context in which that practice takes place.

To think about what forms of social relationships and structures promote human well-being is clearly a huge topic, and is one which requires a much fuller discussion of social and political theory than is possible here. Within this chapter, however, we will begin to explore what it means to think about the good life in relation to the social context within which particular pastoral encounters take place, both at the level of wider society and within specific social institutions.

A Pastoral Response to Domestic Violence: the Case of Deborah

Let us begin this reflection about the social context of pastoral practice with the following case study:

Deborah and her husband, Mike, are both committed members of their local Baptist church. Mike is one of the elders of the congregation, and Deborah has been heavily involved for a number of years in Sunday School teaching and in leading a women's Bible study group. Deborah and Mike have two young children, aged five and three, and most people in their congregation would not think they had any significant difficulties as a family. Deborah does have one or two close friends in the congregation, however, and they have noticed over recent years that she has become more withdrawn and anxious than she used to be.

On one weekday evening, Deborah arrives at the house of her minister. Her face is bruised and she is very distressed. When she has become less upset, she begins to explain that over the past few years Mike has started hitting her. This usually happened when he became angry about something in the church or at home, and this anger would sometimes turn into physical aggression towards her. Mike was always very remorseful after these assaults and would ask Deborah to forgive him. Deborah felt that Mike was so genuinely sorry that it was her Christian duty to forgive him. As time has gone on, these assaults have become more frequent and recently, for the first time, Mike hit her in front of one of their children. Deborah is confused and anxious about what she should do. She believes that it is God's will that she should honour and obey Mike, and that it would be a sin to break her marriage vows by leaving him. At the same time, though, she is becoming increasingly concerned for the safety both of herself and her children. She asks her minister what he thinks she should do.

At this point you might want to think about how you would respond as a pastoral carer in this situation. It is clear from the experiences of some women who have experienced this kind of domestic violence that they have also experienced very inadequate pastoral responses to their situation (see Garma, 1991). Towards the most damaging end of the spectrum of these experiences are occasions in which a pastoral carer's difficulty in acknowledging the abuse and suffering presented to them leads them to deny or minimise the woman's experience. A similar process can occur at a congregational level, when if allegations of abuse are made public, the congregation attempts to deny the validity of these allegations and side with the perpetrator of the abuse (see, for example, Layzell, 1999). Another inadequate response would be the reiteration of scriptural and theological principles (such as the importance and sanctity of the marriage vow), in a way that does not fully face up to the reality of the degree of suffering and danger experienced by the person experiencing the violence (Broadus, 1996).

If we take a regard for the 'Other' and for personal authenticity to be important components of the good life, then it is clear that Deborah is far from experiencing the good life in her current situation. Her relationship with Mike is one in which her personal integrity and authenticity is under sustained attack, to the extent where her very physical well-being is in danger. Furthermore, as outsiders to this relationship, it will seem clear to us that Mike's attitude towards Deborah is far from being one of a deep regard for the 'Other.' If we take personal authenticity and regard for the 'Other' as important markers of the good life, then it is evident that we will be hoping for a change in this situation. This change might either be one in which Mike shows greater regard for Deborah (and his family) and genuinely shifts from his abusive attitudes and behaviour, or in which Deborah and the children find another home environment in which they can be safe and supported. A pastoral response guided by these values will therefore seek to demonstrate regard for Deborah as 'Other', through the offer of an empathic and supportive relationship in which Deborah's experience is taken seriously. Valuing personal authenticity would also tend to lead the pastoral worker to respect Deborah's decision to stay within, or to leave, her marriage. This should not be a naïve attitude, however, and it would be important for a pastoral worker to recognise that Deborah will find it hard to reach a free and authentic decision until she has been able to reflect on the deeply ingrained feelings and beliefs that make it hard for her to contemplate separation from Mike.

Our discussion of Deborah's situation could begin and end with thinking about it at a purely interpersonal level. We could thus focus on key issues for the individuals involved here, such as what leads Mike to act in this violent way or what would be the best resolution for each of the people involved in this situation? Similarly we could think about the pastoral response in terms of how the pastoral worker might best respond to the people involved in this case. Indeed research by Johnson (1995, see also Johnson & Bondurant, 1995) indicates that pastoral carers do tend to think about situations of domestic violence in these interpersonal terms. In particular, Johnson found that pastoral workers tend to attribute the causes of domestic violence to individual, psychological factors (for example, the abusive partner is alcoholic, suffering from stress or has had an emotionally unhealthy upbringing).

Whilst there is value in thinking about instances of domestic violence in terms of these interpersonal or psychological factors, the question raised at the beginning of this chapter encourages us to think about the wider social context in which domestic violence takes place. It is clear in Deborah's immediate situation that Mike's violence towards her is damaging to her well-being. But is it possible that there are wider social influences in this case which are impeding Deborah's ability to experience the good life?

Whilst there are dissenting voices amongst researchers, it is generally agreed that serious acts of domestic violence are more commonly, though not exclusively, perpetrated by men on women (see Kantor & Jasinski, 1998)[1]. This observation has led a number of feminist writers to argue that this violence is not a consequence of random interpersonal factors, but that it reflects wider social patterns involving gender and power. More specifically, feminist writers have proposed that this violence is indicative of a wider social system of *patriarchy*. Bloomquist defines patriarchy in the following way:

> Patriarchy is the complex of ideologies and structures that sustains and perpetuates male control over females. This historically created gender hierarchy of males over females functions as if it were natural. Patriarchy becomes a moral system in which power or control over is the central value not only in male-female relationships but throughout the social and natural order. (Bloomquist 1989: 62)

In other words, patriarchy is the whole network of social symbols, ideas, structures and processes which enables one group to exert power or control over another. Typically this power relationship has taken the form of men exerting control over women, and the concept of patriarchy as an 'ideology' alludes to the different ways in which this hierarchy is depicted as necessary, natural or inevitable. Patriarchy can be seen to be linked to domestic violence in the sense that patriarchal ideas make it seem legitimate for men to exercise control over women and, within cultures where notions of masculinity are associated with aggression, the exertion of this power can thus take violent means. Diane Russell describes this relationship in the following way:

> The primary cause of violence in this country is related to notions that connect masculinity and violence, plus the power imbalance between the sexes that allows men to act out this dangerous connection. For it to be considered unmanly to be powerful, dominant, or violent, great changes will have to be made. (Russell, cited in Bloomquist, 1989: 62)

According to this argument domestic violence is not simply a consequence of individual psychology (or psychopathology), but is an expression of wider social ideas that encourage men to dominate women and to be prepared to express this domination in violent ways. If we accept this analysis of the social factors that encourage domestic violence, then it is evident that pastoral practice will properly focus not only on individual work with perpetrators and survivors of domestic violence, but also on social symbols, practices and structures that nurture this violence. A full and appropriate pastoral practice in response to domestic violence would thus consist not only of care for the individuals involved, but also of reflection and challenge to wider patriarchal influences in the histories, practices and theologies of religious organisations (see, for example, Radford Ruether, 1989; Adams & Fortune, 1995). Such reflection might, for example, take the specific form of asking what the relationship is between liturgy and domestic violence, and seek to identify and challenge particular liturgical forms that validate hierarchical power structures and which value maleness over the female. This reflection could lead into concrete ideas about what it would mean to develop liturgical practices that address and heal experiences of domestic violence and challenge the social influences that give rise to these experiences (see, for example, Procter-Smith, 1995). Similarly pastoral care in relation to domestic violence might also take the form of a critique of wider structures and practices within society that privilege men over women, encourage hierarchical rather than reciprocal relationships and associate healthy masculinity with violence and aggression (see, for example, Bohn, 1989).

Whilst not all readers will necessarily agree with the idea that domestic violence is an expression of patriarchal ideas and structures within wider society, this kind of analysis of the social causes of individual suffering has a clear relevance for our discussion here. For if we think about pastoral care as religiously-motivated practice that is intended to promote the good life, then it becomes clear that pastoral care needs not only to address the painful experiences of individuals but also the social forces that hinder those individuals from experiencing what it means to live well. The theoretical concept of 'patriarchy' thus represents a good case example of how our thinking about what promotes or hinders our experience of the good life needs to take account of wider social symbols, structures or practices that may be damaging. Moral reflection in relation to pastoral practice cannot stop at an analysis of purely individual issues and concerns but needs to take account of wider social factors that promote or impede human well-being. This point will now be further developed in relation to another case study.

The Institutional Context of Pastoral Care: the Case of Tom

Tom is a 76 year-old man who has recently been admitted into hospital after falling at home. Tom never married and has no children or close family. He is a member of a local church, however, and knows a number of people in that congregation. A couple of families in the church are particularly close to him and visit him, or invite him to their homes, on a regular basis.

While he is in hospital, the families that he knows in the local community, and the minister of his church, make contact with the ward sister and the hospital social work department to express their concern about Tom being discharged back home to his flat. They explain that Tom has become increasingly frail over the past few months and that he fell a few weeks ago, but did not need to go into hospital on that occasion. They have also become concerned about his ability to look after himself, as he has become increasingly unkempt. He also seems more confused about his money and a couple of months ago incurred a large debt with a mail order company which he had difficulty repaying.

One of the hospital social workers goes to talk with Tom and explains that his friends are concerned about the idea of him returning home. She asks Tom how he feels he has been managing, and Tom recognises that he has found things more of a struggle. He makes it clear that he really wants to go back to his flat – he has lived there for nearly forty years and would like to be able to live there for the remainder of his life.

The next day Tom's situation is discussed at the ward meeting. His medical tests have shown that he fell because he had suffered from a very slight stroke and he would need to spend around three weeks longer in hospital for rehabilitation before he could return home. The social worker explains that a place has unexpectedly become available in one of the local elderly residential homes and that Tom could be placed there in the next week if he agreed to this. The medical staff want Tom discharged from hospital as soon as possible because there is a high demand for beds on his ward. The social worker agrees to talk to Tom about moving to this residential home. When she does so, she is surprised to find that Tom has changed his mind and that he is prepared to do this rather than return home. 'I don't want to be a burden on other people,' he explains, 'and if my friends and minister don't think I can manage in my flat then maybe I should go into a home.'

The day before Tom is due to go into this residential home, he asks to see the hospital chaplain. When the chaplain arrives, Tom breaks down in tears and explains that whilst he really wants to go home to his flat, other people don't think he can manage by himself and he doesn't want to make life harder for them. Tom is unhappy, but resigned to moving to the residential home.

Again you might want to pause for a moment and think about how you would respond as a pastoral carer in this situation. It is possible, as with the previous case example in this chapter, to think about a response in purely individual terms. At an individual level, the pastoral carer might attempt to empathise with Tom's grief at the loss of his flat, and all that it represents to him, and try to make him feel less isolated in his grief. Or the pastoral carer might want to try to act as an advocate for Tom and to represent his feelings to the health-care team. As with the case example earlier in this chapter, though, there is real value in thinking about Tom's experience in terms of the wider social and institutional context within which it takes place.

First, we can think about the significance of the institutional setting in which Tom's story takes place. The majority of pastoral care takes place in some kind of institutional setting, whether that institution is a church, a hospital, a prison, or an educational organisation. Acknowledging the institutional context of pastoral care adds another layer to our analysis of pastoral encounters, and raises another set of questions about what helps or hinders people in encountering the good life. For example, it is helpful to recognise that institutions generally hold explicit and implicit understandings of their particular nature and social function. Increasingly these understandings might take the explicit form of mission statements, or other policy documents, that set out what the institution hopes to achieve and the means by which it hopes to achieve these ends (Pattison, 1997). Alongside these may be other aims and processes that are far more implicit or even unconscious (Menzies Lyth, 1988). The processes by which institutions decide on these goals, and the degree to which people within institutions actually sympathise with and attempt to achieve these objectives, are clearly complex issues (see, for example, Reed, 1992). At this point in our discussion it is worth making the rather straightforward observation that the goals that institutions pursue, and in particular the means that institutions use to pursue them, do not always promote well-being – and can at times be actively damaging – for individuals within those organisations.

This observation was effectively demonstrated in Erving Goffman's (1961) classic study of institutions entitled *Asylums*. In this book, Goffman focused on what he called 'total institutions', namely organisations in which people lead enclosed lives shut off from wider society – such as prisons, psychiatric institutions, religious orders, nursing homes or army camps. In part of his study, Goffman explored how individuals become accepted and absorbed into these institutions and how they pursue a 'career' within them. One of the basic and striking observations of Goffman's work is that, to achieve their aims, these 'total institutions' engage in practices that dehumanise and disempower individuals within them. For example, he comments:

> The recruit comes into the establishment with a conception of himself [sic] made possible by certain stable arrangements in his home world. Upon entrance, he is immediately stripped of the support provided by these arrangements. In the accurate language of some of our oldest total institutions, he begins a series of abasements, degradations, humiliations, and profanations of self. His self is systematically, if often unintentionally, mortified. (1961: 24)

Specific examples of such 'mortifications' include being placed under restrictions of freedom of movement and ownership of property, being stripped of evidence of one's former 'pre-institutional' identity and finding oneself unable to avoid experiences or people that one would normally find threatening or disturbing. Whilst each of these mortifications can clearly be distressing for the individual experiencing them, they can actually have a useful function for institutions that want to encourage compliance amongst their members so that the overall aim of the institution can be achieved.

Although Goffman's study clearly focused on a particular type of institution, the basic observation that institutional processes can be harmful to individuals can be seen as valid for a much wider range of organisations. Thus, for example, in a health-care system driven by market forces and a primary desire for economic efficiency, the uniqueness and 'Otherness' of individual patients can be neglected. A recent study on values in the contemporary National Health Service included the following story:

> A middle manager described how she was involved in a project to move some continuing care patients from an NHS ward into the private sector. She went to a meeting at the health authority and listened to the decision being made about what should happen to these patients. She said that she understood the need to make a financial decision. However, she was shocked by the way 'they talked about these patients as if they were packets of frozen peas'. (Malby & Pattison, 1999: 11)

In a system of health provision strongly influenced by the language of the market-place, patients can easily become depicted as commodities or financial units, and this in turn can contribute to an environment that is less sensitive to the particular needs of patients. Thus in the case of Tom, the desire on the part of the doctors to discharge him as quickly as is safely possible from the ward reflects the pressure of a market-driven institution in which the most efficient use of bed space is a high priority. As with many institutional goals, the desire to use one's resources efficiently in order to benefit as many people as possible is a commendable one. What we can also note here, however, is that institutional goals that we may consider good can also be pursued in ways that are damaging to particular individuals within the institution. Thus, in Tom's situation, the pressure within the hospital to discharge patients as quickly as is safely possible contributes to a situation in which he is discharged in a manner that leaves him profoundly unhappy.

If we think about social factors that impede Tom's experience of the good life, then there are not only institutional dynamics to bear in mind here. As with the issue of domestic violence and patriarchy noted above, it is possible to see some wider social beliefs and ideologies that have a bearing on his case.

The particular set of assumptions that I have in mind here relate to the term 'ageism.' Blytheway (1995) argues that an adequate definition of ageism highlights inappropriate assumptions or practices that may be related to any particular age. More specifically, he proposes the following definition:

> Ageism legitimates the use of chronological age to mark out classes of people who are systematically denied resources and opportunities that others enjoy, and who suffer the consequences of such denigration, ranging from well-meaning patronage to unambiguous vilification. (1995: 14)

Ageism can therefore be evident in the assumptions and practices of employers who regard unemployed people in their forties and fifties to be too old to regard as serious applicants for jobs that they are seeking to fill. Equally ageism can be present in the negative stereotyping of young people. For the case of Tom, however, it is particularly pertinent to think about ageism in terms of negative assumptions and practices that are held in relation to those in later life (see, for example, Pilcher, 1995: 98). The pervasive nature of these negative assumptions is well-illustrated in the following story:

> Mrs S. is 82 and lives in a block of sheltered flats. One morning she was observed by a neighbour walking to the shops at 7.30am, one-and-a-half hours before they opened. The neighbour took her by the arm and led her back to the flat. Ten minutes later the same neighbour saw her walking to the shops once more and took her back to her flat a second time. This time, Mrs S. became disturbed; the GP was called; he prescribed a tranquiliser, and she slept all day. At 5.30pm she walked to the common room of the block of flats to play bingo, which did not start until 7.30pm. She was taken back to her flat by one resident, another came in to make her a cup of tea, a third called the warden, who rang the GP again, and contacted her son. At this point the woman became very disturbed, claiming that people were trying to kill her, and the GP said that he would ask for a second opinion from a consultant psychiatrist. It was then discovered that her son had turned her clock *back* an hour instead of turning it *forward* the previous evening which had been the spring equinox. (Blytheway, 1995: 92)

This story graphically illustrates how for the 'carers' in this situation (and perhaps for us as the audience of this story as well), the apparently unusual behaviour of Mrs S. was quickly interpreted as evidence of dementia or mental incapacity on her part. The association of ageing with physical and psychological decline remains a powerful assumption within contemporary Western culture, and as a consequence those in later life are more likely to experience doubt from others about their competence and capacity for autonomy.

It is reasonable to claim that if we hold negative stereotypes about old age, then it becomes much harder to engage with people in later life in a way in which their uniqueness and 'Otherness' is recognised. Furthermore people in later life can find ageist assumptions working against their ability to live in authentic and autonomous ways. For if we assume that elderly people have decreasing capacities to think and act for themselves, then it becomes easier for individuals and institutions to engage in 'caring' practices that promote what we believe to be for the best for the elderly person, over and against their own wishes. Ageist assumptions can be demonstrated not only by younger people towards those in later life, but also by elderly persons themselves. Thus negative stereotypes about old age can be internalised by people in later life in such a way that they increasingly come to doubt their own abilities as well.

The lack of appropriate, respectful and supportive relationships, as well as factors that impede autonomy, can be seen as two of the most significant barriers to well-being in later life (Bond & Coleman, 1993: 339).

Insofar as ageist assumptions make appropriate and respectful relationships with elderly people harder to achieve, as well as encouraging an environment for caring practices that disempower elderly people, it can therefore be argued that ageism is another social ideology that can impede an experience of the good life. This analysis could certainly be applied to the case of Tom, described above. Whilst it may well be true that Tom was taking care of himself to a less high standard, those in his support network viewed his 'decline' in ageist terms as evidence of a growing incapacity from which he needed to be protected, even if this meant his own wishes were contravened. Tom's internalisation of these negative assumptions about his capacity for autonomy is also arguably evident in the fact that he is prepared to go along with a discharge plan that he is unhappy with, both because he is unsure of himself and because he does not want to cause any trouble for his carers.

Tom's story, thus, can serve as an illustration both of how institutional goals and practices, and wider social ideologies, can impede individuals' ability to experience the good life. In the second case study we can see again how reflection on the moral dimensions of pastoral practice will need to focus not only on individual issues and dilemmas, but on wider social ideas and practices that damage people's well-being. In Tom's case, a pastoral worker may well feel that they will want to encourage those making decisions about Tom's future to reflect more on ageist assumptions which they may be making about him. Furthermore, pastoral practice in relation to the care of the elderly might also take the form of challenging inappropriate or disempowering practices at an institutional level, or might take the form of education or campaigning work that seeks to challenge negative stereotypes of old age. This kind of pastoral practice can be understood as 'prophetic' (Gerkin, 1991), in the sense that it moves beyond a concern purely for the individual case to a wider challenging of social and institutional ideas and practices. Clearly such 'prophetic' pastoral practice will involve engaging with complex social and structural issues. In the case of Tom, there are genuine questions as to what priority can be given to his desire to return home when this will prevent another person from making use of his hospital bed. Equally, questions can be asked as to whether the dilemma of choosing between giving bed space to Tom or another patient is itself a symptom of injustice in terms of the underfunding of health resources. What is being advocated in this chapter is not a simplistic approach to analysing complex social issues (though the brevity of the discussion here could unintentionally encourage this). Rather, what I argue for primarily is simply the importance of taking account of the social and institutional context in which pastoral encounters take place, and of thinking critically about those elements within that social context that are harmful to human well-being.

Summary

It is important to recognise that running through the discussion here has been the theme of power. Power is an intrinsic element of all human relationships and the appropriate expression of power is an integral part of healthy communities and relationships (see Poling, 1991: 23). Equally, the abuse of power is evident when individuals, social groups and institutions act in ways that disregard the humanity or 'Otherness' of those who are more vulnerable or who lack the resources to protect themselves. The two case studies discussed in this chapter both concerned issues of power. The first involved Mike's physical and psychological power to hurt Deborah, which could be interpreted as reflecting wider social and religious ideas and structures that give men power over women. The second case involved the power of those involved in Tom's care to coerce him into making decisions with which he was deeply unhappy. Again, this power reflected the institutional power of the hospital and the wider power given to younger people by ageist stereotypes to make decisions on behalf of those in later life. When thinking about what helps or hinders people's ability to experience the good life, it is therefore important to be particularly attentive to issues of power and to ask critical questions about whether power is being expressed in particular pastoral encounters in ways that promote or damage human well-being. The theme of power is a central one in analysing moral aspects of pastoral encounters, and it is one that we will return to in the next chapter.

Notes

1   For a helpful discussion, from a feminist perspective, of violence perpetrated by women, see Kelly, 1996.

5

The boundaries of the pastoral relationship

So far, we have explored the idea that all pastoral practice is shaped by the pastoral worker's understanding of the good life. This idea has led on to discussions of how we try to identify the values that influence our practice, and how we can reflect on the adequacy of our vision of the good life. In the previous chapter, we turned our attention to the question of whether different dimensions of the pastoral encounter actually help or hinder people's ability to experience the good life. Our focus there was on the social context in which the pastoral encounter takes place, and we noted the importance of pastoral practitioners thinking critically about social and institutional factors that limit people's ability to live well.

It is not only within the wider social context of pastoral care that damaging ideas or practices can be identified, however. The way in which individual pastoral relationships are themselves structured and conducted will have a deeply significant bearing on whether recipients of pastoral care are helped to a greater experience of well-being or not. Indeed there is a growing awareness in the literature on pastoral care that pastoral relationships have the potential to be extremely damaging.

This potential for harm is illustrated in the following story of Susan. Susan had been sexually abused for much of her early childhood, and continues her story at the point where the abuse had been disclosed to others:

> I felt terrible, I felt like everybody blamed me. The only person who seemed to care was this young priest, Father Greg. He listened to me, and said the right things. He was great with me…. I could talk to him about anything, I really loved him. We stayed great friends for years. When I was going to get married he seemed really against it and warned me off, which I thought was a bit odd. But he brought us a wedding present. Then he was sent back to Ireland for two years, and I didn't see him during that time. After I was married, and he had come back from Ireland, he came to visit us. We hadn't seen each other for ages, and we sat up talking until late at night, after my husband had gone to bed. When we got up to go to bed, it was late as we'd been talking and talking, and he said, 'Can I have a goodnight kiss?' I thought, 'What's he on about?' He'd never even hugged me, never mind wanted to kiss

me, all the time I'd known him. So I went over to give him a quick kiss on the cheek, and that's not the way he kissed me at all, and it terrified me and I pulled away, and he just kept a hold of me. I thought, 'Oh God, what's happening?' I wasn't frightened of him, it was the fact that he was a priest, that was all that was in my mind: 'They don't do this, this doesn't happen with priests.' (Cashman, 1993: 21)

In her story Susan then goes on to recount another occasion in which this priest made sexual advances towards her, and then she continues:

It seemed to be, that I'd taken my problems to him when I was younger, and he'd helped me, and I really needed him, and I was grateful – but now it was payback time. I hadn't understood there would be a price to pay, but there was. I did love him for his kindness, and I needed to talk to him, but I didn't want sex with him. But he made me feel I owed it to him. Before all this, I'd always felt very safe with priests. Not any more…. I felt that terrible and guilty, I can't tell you. Sometimes I feel like shaking him and yelling, 'Do you know what you did to me?' (Cashman, 1993: 22f.)

It is evident that this experience of a pastoral relationship has been a very damaging one for Susan. The support she received from Father Greg – and the important step she took in trusting a male authority figure – had been compromised by his desire to have sex with her. This has undermined not only the consolation and support she experienced from Father Greg, but also her ability to accept care from other pastoral workers in the future. Susan's story illustrates clearly how some pastoral relationships can actually impede people's experience of the good life. Certainly we may question the extent to which Father Greg's attitude here is genuinely one of regard for Susan's 'Otherness'.

In this chapter and the next, we will examine what elements of individual pastoral relationships can help or hinder the well-being of those who receive pastoral care and counselling. In the next chapter, we will focus on what qualities of the pastoral relationship itself are important in helping people to move closer toward the good life. For now, we will examine the notion of the boundaries of the pastoral relationship and reflect on the role of boundaries in the promotion of the good life through pastoral practice.

The Significance of Boundaries in Pastoral Relationships

Towards the end of the last chapter we noted the idea that power is inseparable from human relationships. If we think of power as the capacity of individuals and groups to act in relation to themselves and each other, then it is clear that our existence is framed by a network of relationships in which we exercise power towards others and experience their power on our own selves. This network of power need not be thought about in negative terms – indeed the creative, empathic and benevolent use of this power in our relationships is integral to our psychological and spiritual growth. Or to use the concepts we have referred to before in this book, the appropriate use of power in human relations is an integral part of allowing the expression of personal authenticity and showing proper regard to the 'Other'.

It is evident, though, that the power that is present between individuals, groups and social institutions can be used in ways that are physically, psychologically and spiritually damaging. Just as human relationships have the capacity to be creative and nurturing, so they also have the potential to be destructive and abusive. In relationships where one partner is significantly more powerful than the other, the more powerful party has greater potential for acting in ways that are destructive for the other person than in relationships where power is more evenly shared. Where such power imbalances exists in human relationships, it is useful to think in terms of limits or boundaries that are placed on the actions of the more powerful partner to protect the vulnerability of the weaker one. In this context, boundaries can therefore serve to clarify what kinds of actions are appropriate, and which are likely to be damaging, within particular relationships. For example, given that adults have the power to harm children through physical, emotional or sexual abuse, it is important that certain limits are set on how adults can act towards children. Similarly in adult relationships, where one party is dependent upon or weaker than the other in some way, it is important that clear boundaries are set that prevent the more powerful partner from exploiting the weaker party for their own benefit. The concept of boundaries is therefore an important one in maintaining appropriate expressions of power within human relationships. Indeed there is reasonable evidence to suggest that some people who engage in abusive acts towards children and adults do have difficulty in maintaining appropriate boundaries more generally in their personal or professional relationships (Poling, 1991: 69; Russell, 1993).

Boundaries serve an important function in pastoral relationships, precisely because there is often a power imbalance in such relationships with one person offering care (and often holding a particular institutional status) and the other, to at least some degree, needing this support. We can see this power imbalance clearly in the case of Susan and Father Greg. Susan was the more vulnerable person in the relationship as she needed Greg's emotional help and support, whereas Greg held more power as the person who had the ability to give, withhold, or bargain with, his support. Susan's degree of dependency on Greg meant that he was able to seek to exploit her vulnerability to meet his own desires. He could then act in ways that contradicted her interests and it was harder for Susan to resist his sexual advances precisely because she was dependent on his help.

Thinking about the notion of appropriate boundaries in pastoral relationships is a complex task. Partly this is because pastoral work takes place in such a wide variety of settings and involves a wide range of relationships, and partly because many pastoral relationships take place in congregational contexts in which the boundaries of the pastoral worker's relationships with others are easily blurred. As the case of Susan demonstrates, it is important for us to think carefully about what constitutes appropriate boundaries for pastoral practice if we are to avoid the kind of harm that she experienced in her contact with Father Greg.

When reflecting on the appropriate boundaries of the pastoral relationship, it can be useful to begin by exploring which kinds of boundaries are necessary to enable a pastoral relationship to function effectively. Our thinking on this issue can be helped by referring to the notion of the 'therapeutic frame' (Boyd & Lynch, 1999). Anne Gray (1994) has described the therapeutic frame as the system of boundaries that are needed to enable counselling and psychotherapy relationships to function effectively. Gray suggests that in the same way that a painting requires a frame in order to focus the viewer's attention on it, so a therapeutic relationship needs a clear set of boundaries in place in order for the therapist and client to be able to focus in depth on the client's experience.

The key qualities of this therapeutic frame are *transparency* and *consistency*. Thus the therapeutic frame should consist of boundaries that are clear to both the therapist and their client. This clarity is usually achieved by the therapist and client agreeing on a contract together at the outset of their relationship concerning the basis on which they would work together. This contract would, for example, typically include an understanding of the location, length and frequency of the counselling sessions, of the financial cost of the counselling (including charges for missed sessions), and of the degree of confidentiality that the counsellor could offer to the client. The transparency of the therapeutic frame can also be helped by professional codes of ethics which make clear the terms on which counsellors and psychotherapists work with clients, and which explicitly prohibit the exploitation of therapeutic relationships for the emotional, financial or sexual benefit of the therapist (see, for example, British Association for Counselling and Psychotherapy, 2001). The consistency of the therapeutic frame is achieved through observing the terms of the contract, and by not acting against this contract unless this is renegotiated between the counsellor and client. The therapeutic contract should set down clearly the terms on which the therapeutic relationship would be conducted, and these terms should be consistently maintained as the relationship progresses. Furthermore the therapist should consistently relate to the client within the boundaries set down in their professional code of ethics.

The concept of the therapeutic frame is a helpful one for focusing our attention on what boundaries are necessary for a therapeutic relationship to function effectively. Proponents of this idea argue that without a consistent approach to the length of counselling sessions or a clear agreement about the limits of confidentiality in a counselling relationship, it becomes harder for the client to feel safe to explore their thoughts and feelings in depth. A clear therapeutic frame provides the client with a clear and consistent framework within which they can explore painful or shameful aspects of their experience, whereas unclear boundaries for a therapeutic relationship can leave a client feeling more out of control and less prepared to risk exposing themselves within the relationship.

Whilst the notion of the 'therapeutic frame' in counselling and psychotherapy relationships provides some clear ideas about the nature of appropriate boundaries in this context, applying this concept to pastoral relationships can be more complex. Transparency and consistency may well be important elements of the therapeutic frame, but in many pastoral relationships it may be difficult to apply these concepts. Many pastoral encounters take place in relatively unstructured ways, such as through irregular home visits or conversations before or after religious services. Given the informal nature of these contacts, it would often feel inappropriate and cumbersome for the pastoral worker to set out a clear contract of how often they would visit a particular person, or for how long these visits would last. The boundaries that the pastoral carer brings to these informal conversations are therefore generally left implicit. Although the person they meet with may well assume that the pastoral carer will not act in ways that are harmful to them, the specific boundaries that the pastoral carer places on their work are not usually transparent. Similarly, the informal setting of much pastoral practice means that consistency may also be difficult to achieve. The pastoral carer is unlikely to see those that they work with for set periods of time, nor might they even see them in the same place or even for the same reason or in the same role. An important part of pastoral work, whether in congregational or chaplaincy settings, does seem to be the capacity of the pastoral worker to respond in a flexible way to the situations that they encounter.

Does the concept of the 'therapeutic frame' really have anything to offer then to our understanding of boundaries in pastoral practice? I believe that it does for two reasons. First, I think an understanding of the 'therapeutic frame' can help us to begin to distinguish between different types of pastoral work in which different kinds of boundaries are appropriate. More specifically, I think it can be useful to distinguish between 'pastoral counselling', as a particular form of pastoral practice based on a clear therapeutic frame, and 'pastoral care' as a broader type of pastoral activity which involves a more flexible approach to boundaries. If we follow this distinction, then we will see 'pastoral counselling' as a pastoral relationship based on a professional counselling model, in which the pastoral counsellor negotiates a clear contract with their client at the outset of the counselling and maintains this consistent therapeutic frame throughout their work together. Pastoral care, on the other hand, would be seen as a more fluid type of work, often utilising 'counselling skills', with a more flexible approach to the timing, location and the nature of the contact that the pastoral practitioner would have with those with whom they worked. The advantage of the more formal pastoral counselling approach is that it would provide a clear and consistent framework in which clients could explore their thoughts and feelings in depth over a period of time. The advantage of the more fluid pastoral care model is that it allows pastoral workers to respond in flexible ways to the different situations and relationships in which they find themselves. The idea of the therapeutic frame can help us to begin to think about whether there are different types of pastoral work that require different degrees of boundary flexibility or clarity.

A second sense in which the idea of the therapeutic frame can be useful is in terms of highlighting the kinds of boundaries that pastoral workers need to think about in relation to their work. We noted earlier that the therapeutic frame involves an understanding about the boundaries of the time, location and duration of counselling sessions, as well as about the limits of confidentiality for that relationship. Other aspects of the frame include an understanding of the limits of the therapeutic relationship (for example, that it will not also function as a friendship, or as a sexual or business relationship) and support systems such as clinical supervision that enable this frame to be kept in place. Given these elements of the therapeutic frame, we could ask the following questions about the appropriate boundaries of pastoral care:

- Are there certain times when it is generally inappropriate for pastoral work to take place?
- Are there certain places or circumstances where it is inappropriate for pastoral work to take place?
- What are the appropriate boundaries of confidentiality for pastoral relationships?
- Are there certain kinds of contact or relationship with another person that are incompatible with a pastoral role towards them?
- Are there certain kinds of action towards another person that are incompatible with a pastoral role towards them?
- What resources do pastoral carers have to help them think about these boundary issues in relation to their work?

In general, pastoral workers have often found themselves left to reflect on these issues by themselves. Informal guidance may have been found through conversations with other pastoral workers, but more formal supervision of pastoral practice remains rare in Britain (Lyall, 1995: 69–79). More recently, guidance on these kinds of boundary question has been provided by some religious groups who have produced codes of ethics and practice for pastoral workers. In the remaining part of this chapter, we shall examine the nature and rationale of such codes, as well as their limitations in helping us to think about the appropriate boundaries of pastoral encounters.

The Role of Pastoral Codes of Ethics

Whilst it is essential that individual pastoral workers develop the ability to think for themselves about how best to manage the boundaries in their pastoral relationships, certain difficulties arguably arise if decisions about boundaries are left purely to individual discretion. These difficulties are illustrated in a case example given by Peter Rutter from his own practice as a psychiatrist. Rutter is one of the leading writers to have explored the issue of sexual abuse in the context of professional relationships. In *Sex in the Forbidden Zone* (Rutter, 1989), he explains how his interest in this subject began partly as a result of his growing awareness of colleagues who had sex with their patients, clients or students, and partly out of his own experience with a particular patient, Mia. Rutter describes how, during one therapy session, Mia began to talk of her despair about whether she would ever have a satisfactory relationship with a man and she expressed her despair by slumping from her chair on to the floor. Mia then moved over towards Rutter and touched him on his legs in a way that he realised was becoming increasingly sexual. At this point in his life Rutter himself was feeling lonely and depressed, and was very tempted to allow a sexual encounter to take place between them as a source of comfort to himself. He resisted this temptation, and asked Mia to return to her seat, opening up a valuable conversation between them on the way in which she sought to use sex with men as a means of alleviating her distress.

In the moment of being tempted to have a sexual encounter with Mia, though, Rutter became aware of how powerful the appeal of such an encounter could be. Reflecting on this experience, he comments:

> To me, and to all men in power, the woman can easily become a sympathetic, wounded, vulnerable presence who admires and needs us in an especially feminine way. If we have been working together for some time, a familiarity and trust develops between us that starts to erode the boundaries of seemingly impersonal professional relationships.... As a result, we may find ourselves experiencing a closeness, a comfort, a sense of *completeness* with these women

that we have long sought but rarely found.... Under these conditions, images of sexual union flood us. The rule forbidding sexual contact with these women can seem hazy and distant, no longer applicable. We long to be free of the special obligations that prohibit sexual expression of our feelings for each other. In the moment, it feels so easy, so magical, so relieving for us to cross the invisible boundary and merge with the woman in shared passion. (Rutter, 1989: 8)

Rutter's story illustrates the point that, whilst an individual may believe in principle that certain boundaries should be upheld in their professional relationships, their commitment to such principles can be severely tested in particular situations. His experience shows how inappropriate sexual contact with a patient or client can seem deeply appealing as a source of comfort or intimacy, especially when these may be otherwise lacking in a person's life. In the face of such appeal, it is easier to see how professionals can rationalise sexual misconduct as somehow a positive or healing experience for both themselves and for their client.

Although the discussion here so far has been specifically focused on the breach of sexual boundaries between professionals and their patients, clients or students, the points raised are relevant not only to sexual boundaries. Although psychiatrists, lecturers, doctors and priests may have a clear notion of what constitutes appropriate boundaries with those with whom they work, it is precisely at those points where they are vulnerable (whether emotionally, sexually or financially) that they may be tempted to exploit their professional relationships to meet their own needs. Furthermore, such exploitation may become shrouded in self-deception as the professional worker interprets their breach of boundaries as something positive, such as an expression of friendship, love or mutuality.

Whilst it is important that pastoral workers do maintain an ability to make their own decisions about the boundaries of their pastoral relationships, it is evident that making these decisions in appropriate ways is not an easy process. Most pastoral workers will experience periods of their working life in which they feel drained, lonely, unappreciated or depressed. During these periods it can be tempting to seek solace from those with whom one has pastoral relationships, even if this means acting in ways that are not wholly appropriate to a pastoral encounter. This pressure can be even stronger for pastoral workers based in congregational settings where the distinction between the pastoral relationship and friendship can be less clear. In the face of such pressure, pastoral practitioners can find themselves rationalising actions and kinds of relationship that are actually unhelpful to those with whom they work (see Lynch, 1999b).

Given that it may be difficult for individuals always to make appropriate choices about the boundaries in their professional relationships, this provides one possible rationale for the creation of codes of ethics and standards which make clear the appropriate limits of these relationships.

A written code which sets out the standards of practice that are expected in a particular profession can provide a reference point against which individuals can evaluate their own practice. Thus, if individual judgment can at times be clouded by self-interest, formal codes of ethics and standards can make it clear what kinds of actions are prohibited to the person bound by that code, even when that course of action might be deeply tempting to them.

One proposed function of professional codes of ethics is not simply to provide a framework against which individual workers can judge their practice. A range of other reasons exist for the creation of such codes in terms of benefits to the particular profession as a whole and to the wider public. Thus professional codes of ethics and standards can also serve the function of:

- Providing a reference point for the public in general, and for users of the professional relationship in particular, which can enable them to be clear about the basis on which that professional relationship will be conducted
- Enabling professional malpractice to be identified and for those who contravene the standards set out in the code to be disciplined in some way by their professional body (for example, by expulsion from that body)
- Providing a focus and stimulus for ongoing discussion within a given profession on what constitutes ethical practice
- Clarifying points where professional practice touches upon legal issues, and to identify forms of practice which may break the law.

The creation of professional codes of ethics can therefore be motivated by a desire to give guidance to professionals themselves, to protect those who use that professional service, and to protect the public standing of that profession by providing a structure for sanctioning those who bring the profession into disrepute.

The creation of codes of ethics for pastoral workers is still at a relatively early stage compared to many other professions, with codes often being created more at a local (e.g. diocesan) level, rather than at a national level as with other professional groups. One example of such a code is the Diocese of Oxford's (1996) *Code of Ministerial Practice*. This document begins with an introductory section which explains, the general purpose of codes of ethics and practice and the rationale for developing such a code to identify good standards of pastoral practice. This section also identifies those to whom the code should apply, namely 'all those who exercise a recognised ministry within the Church' within that diocese (ibid: 6). In common with other professional codes (see, for example, British Association for Counselling and Psychotherapy, 2001), this document then moves into a section of general points about its purpose and application (Section A of the code). It states that its guidelines are 'to be applied sensitively and imaginatively to different roles and circumstances' (Diocese of Oxford, 1996: 12). Furthermore, the document exhorts ordained and lay ministers to encourage the good standards of pastoral practice set out in the code within the congregations or other groups that they work with. A general point is also made about the importance of the creative and open use of the power held by pastoral workers, and of observing proper boundaries in pastoral relationships.

These general comments about the nature and purpose of the code then lead into more specific guidelines both for 'good ministerial practice' (Section B of the code), for 'pastoral care' (Section C of the code) and for 'confidentiality' (Section D of the code). Examples of the guidelines for 'good ministerial practice' are:

B3 Ministers must:

3.1 Behave at all times in a way that is not detrimental to the communication of the Gospel in word and deed. Behaviour should be such as to enhance and embody the communication of the Gospel.

3.2 Act in such a way as to uphold and enhance the good standing of the Church as a body concerned with the pastoral care and well-being of others.

3.3 Act in such a way as to justify and maintain public trust and confidence in accredited ministers of the Church.

3.4 Seek the good of the parishioners and others in their pastoral care, and those over whom they exercise a supervisory relationship.

3.5 Take responsibility for their own ongoing training and development.

3.6 Decline any duties or responsibilities which are beyond their proper competence.

3.7 Make opportunities for ministry available to others and assist others in discerning their vocation.

B4   Ministers should not:

4.1   Undertake any 'professional' duties whilst under the influence of alcohol or drugs.

4.2   Abuse the privileged relationship between minister and parishioner, nor abuse the privileged access this gives them to a person, their home, property or workplace. Nor should ministers abuse the privileged relationship between themselves and colleagues or trainees.

4.3   Deal with church finances in such a way that the distinction between personal and church monies becomes blurred.

4.4   Enter into or continue any pastoral relationship with the purpose of receiving any personal advantage or gain, whether monetary, emotional, sexual or material.

4.5   Seek to represent a personal opinion or viewpoint as the official stand or teaching of the Church. (1996: 14–5)

The section on guidelines for pastoral care includes the following:

C3   Those engaged in pastoral ministry should:

3.1   Recognise the importance of their own devotional life as the foundation of Christian pastoral care.

3.2   Be aware of the necessity to behave in a competent, professional and ethical manner.

3.3   Be aware of the necessity to seek support in the work they are doing. A minister should always be ready to seek further help and appropriate training.

C4   In any pastoral relationship, ministers should:

4.1   Be aware both of their own emotional needs and the vulnerability of the other person.

4.2   Act with compassion whilst keeping a proper emotional and psychological distance.

4.3   Be clear what sort of help or advice is being sought. It is the minister's responsibility to work towards a clear understanding by all parties of the sort of help being sought and offered.

4.4   Be clear about what they are able and competent to offer.

4.5 Be aware of the necessity to bring different phases of a pastoral relationship to a conclusion. Pastoral relationships should encourage maturity and growth, not dependency.

C5 Responding to pastoral needs in a professional manner means paying attention to:

5.1 The place and timing of a meeting and its duration.
5.2 Whether the fact of a meeting is known to others. (There is a distinction between confidentiality and secrecy).
5.3 Whether the meeting is to be of a formal or informal nature, and what records are to be kept.
5.4 The atmosphere of the place of meeting, including the arrangement of furniture and lighting.

C6 Situations ministers should avoid include:

6.1 Visiting someone alone at home late at night, or encouraging someone to visit the minister when they are alone at home late at night.
6.2 Spending time with a child or children in a place that is quite separate from other people.
6.3 A long-term pastoral relationship with one person in a partnership, when a significant part of the pastoral care focuses upon difficulties in the marriage/partner relationship. In these circumstances the minister should seek to work with the couple wherever possible. (1996: 16–17).

In the final section of the code, guidelines on maintaining confidentiality are presented, such as assuming that personal information divulged by parishioners is to be treated as confidential, only sharing confidential information about a parishioner with others with their consent (unless the parishioner is at risk of harming themselves or others), and trying to maintain parishioners' anonymity when discussing their situations in supervisory or training conditions.

It is possible to see codes such as this one in a positive way, or to adopt a more critical view of them. On the positive side, a code such as this can highlight issues that pastoral workers need to reflect on in relation to their practice, such as the way in which they use power in their pastoral relationships, the limits of their pastoral role and competence, and the appropriate timing, context and content of pastoral interventions. A code of ethics can therefore provide a framework for reflection, as pastoral practitioners explore the significance of the code's broad guidelines for the specific situations in which they find themselves in their work. Furthermore, it could be argued that the code can also give clear guidance as to what kinds of activities are incompatible with good ministerial and pastoral practice, and in so doing, hopefully reinforce pastoral workers' understanding of what constitutes good or bad practice.

At the same time, however, the extracts from this particular code also suggest some of the limitations of codes of ethics and practice more generally. For example, this code contains a number of positive attitudes that pastoral workers are encouraged to aspire to. These include acting in ways that enhance the communication of the Gospel, that promote the good standing of the Church and that promote the well-being of those in the pastoral worker's care. These general aspirations are neatly summarised in section C3.2 of the code which emphasises the necessity of acting in a 'competent, professional and ethical' manner. Now if we assume that bad pastoral practice is only conducted by people who are intentionally cruel, malicious or negligent then general exhortations to be 'good' in one's practice may have some value. But if we accept that bad pastoral practice may very often be conducted by people who are well-intentioned but insensitive or unreflective about the implications of their work, then general encouragement to be a 'good' practitioner may have little positive effect. A pastoral worker may be motivated by intentions that they see as good, whilst engaging in practice that is actually damaging to those with whom they work. Codes of ethics which include general exhortations to 'good' practice will actually do little to promote genuinely good practice unless they can help practitioners think more specifically about what 'good' or 'bad' practice actually is.

A second limitation evident in this code concerns what kinds of actions are prohibited within it. Whilst this code contains some clear and specific guidelines on the types of actions which are incompatible with good pastoral work, there are inevitably questions about why these actions are chosen over others. In this code, the actions that tend to be specifically prohibited are those associated with financial, sexual or relational impropriety on the part of the pastoral worker. It is evident that these kinds of actions are precisely those that tend to open the Church to critical public and media scrutiny. The exploitation of pastoral relationships for personal gain (whether financial, sexual or emotional) is without doubt a very significant source of harm in pastoral practice, but it can be argued that ill-timed, insensitive and morally judgmental pastoral responses are also generally damaging to care-seekers' well-being. When identifying those actions which are prohibited to pastoral workers, there may be a temptation for codes of ethics to highlight obvious forms of misconduct which are likely to lead to ministers being featured in the pages of the tabloid press, rather than stimulating more detailed reflection about the kinds of pastoral practice that can be damaging.

One further general objection to the value of professional codes of ethics and practice should also be noted. We have already discussed in this chapter the idea that such codes could help practitioners to reflect about good standards in their practice. A counter-argument is whether in reality such codes enable this to happen or whether they actually become substitutes for effective moral reflection. Stephen Pattison (1999, 2001) makes the point that professional codes often include a mix of, apparently arbitrarily chosen, general ethical principles and specific prohibitions in relation to practice. This framework of arbitrary principles and fixed rules can in fact, he argues, represent more of a block than an aid to developing a thoughtful approach to one's practice. He comments:

> Insofar as codes exact unswerving adherence to their own narrow field of vision and regulation from professional members, they may discourage them from developing and exercising appropriate autonomous ethical judgment. By including an undifferentiated mixture of professional and broader, more philosophical ethical norms, codes may induce a false sense in professional members that, when they are following and obeying the code, they are in fact automatically acting ethically. This, too, might lead to a suspension of individual judgment. In that codes require obedience to some clear norms and precepts, they may encourage professionals to be passive and legalistic rather than actively morally discerning.... Codes can easily become a narrow cage rather than a springboard for responsible ethically informed action. (Pattison, 1999: 379)

This argument by Pattison is helpful in focusing our attention on what is arguably most important in the proper management of the boundaries of pastoral relationships, namely that individual pastoral workers develop an increasing ability to reflect critically on the nature and effects of their practice.

Summary

In this chapter, we have seen how power is inevitably present in pastoral relationships and how appropriate boundaries should be maintained to ensure that the power held by pastoral workers is used in ways that promote others' well-being. Whilst it is possible to identify a range of questions that pastoral practitioners can reflect on in relation to the boundaries of their work, we have also noted that it may be difficult in some situations for pastoral workers to identify by themselves what constitutes good practice and to act on this. This raises the key question of what support structures are necessary to help pastoral carers think critically and ethically about their work. We have explored the notion that professional codes of ethics and practice for pastoral workers may have some role to play here. It is clear, though, that such codes cannot appropriately serve as a replacement for moral reflection but should be written in ways that provide a framework within which moral reflection can take place. Codes of ethics also need to be supplemented by appropriate training and supervision of pastoral practice in which practitioners have the opportunity to develop the skills of reflecting on their work (see, for example, Foskett & Lyall, 1988). Through such supervision and training, pastoral workers may be able to strengthen their own 'internal supervisor' (Casement, 1985, 1990), that is, their own ability to reflect in the midst of pastoral situations about what would constitute good or bad, helpful or unhelpful, practice in that situation.

The issue of appropriate boundaries in pastoral relationships demands attention if we are to develop pastoral practice that genuinely promotes the good life. As we have seen, this issue leads us not only to think about specific questions about what kinds of relationships or actions are appropriate or inappropriate in pastoral encounters, but also into more general questions about how we can develop and support greater moral and critical reflection amongst individual pastoral practitioners. Further attention to these more general issues is vital in Britain if we are to see the further development of good standards of pastoral care and counselling.

6

Friendship & the qualities of the pastoral relationship

Having explored the significance of the boundaries of the pastoral relationship, it is important to balance this discussion by thinking about what represents important qualities of the relationship between the pastoral carer and care-seeker. Although the maintenance of appropriate boundaries is integral to effective helping relationships, it is also evident that clear boundaries devoid of other human qualities are not therapeutic. Indeed when people who have received counselling and psychotherapy report on what they found most helpful from it, they tend to emphasise qualities such as feeling accepted or understood by the therapist (McLeod, 1990; Howe, 1993). Whilst attention to the appropriate boundaries of pastoral relationships is important in avoiding pastoral encounters that are abusive or damaging, it is also important for us to ask what kind of personal qualities in a pastoral relationship help people to a greater experience of the good life?

In the previous chapter I suggested that the pastoral relationship is a formal helping relationship that is quite distinct from a friendship. The expectations, roles and responsibilities of the pastoral carer and care-seeker are different to those that we would normally observe in a relationship between friends. In this chapter, I want to modify that idea and suggest that the types of pastoral relationships that are most likely to enable people to experience something of the good life are those which contain certain elements of friendship. The way in which these two ideas can be held in tension will hopefully be clear by the end of this chapter.

Initially, we will think about the nature of friendship by briefly exploring the work of one of the most important moral philosophers to write on this subject, Aristotle. Having discussed key elements of Aristotle's understanding of friendship, we will then think about how these translate into a contemporary understanding of the important qualities of the pastoral relationship.

A Classical Understanding of Friendship

One of the striking features of contemporary western society has been the growing importance of friendship. Indeed within postmodern western culture, an individual's network of friends can be as, if not more, important to them than their family ties or partnerships (Pahl, 2000). 'I'll be there for you,' goes the theme tune of one of the most popular TV sitcoms of the past decade, *Friends*, and this phrase expresses the aspiration that one's friends will be a consistently stable and supportive presence in a culture generally characterised by fluidity and change.

Interest in the significance of friendship is far from being simply a contemporary concern. Indeed philosophical reflection on the nature of friendship was undertaken by ancient classical writers such as Plato, Aristotle and Cicero[1]. For our purposes here, Aristotle's discussion of the nature of friendship contains ideas that may be helpful for our understanding of contemporary pastoral relationships, and it is to his work that we will now turn.

In Aristotle's view, experiencing a true friendship with another person is an essential part of the good life. 'No one would choose to live without friends, even if he had all the other goods,' he wrote in his *Nichomachean Ethics* (Aristotle, 2000: 143). For Aristotle, human well-being is fundamentally defined by the desire for a particular quality of relationship with other people. It is important to recognise, though, that when Aristotle wrote about the importance of friendship for the good life, he did not have in mind every kind of relationship that might fit the label 'friendship'. Rather Aristotle identified three different types of 'friendship', two of which he saw as inferior to the ideal 'friendship of virtue' that was integral to the good life.

The types of friendship that Aristotle saw as being more inferior were what he described as 'friendships of utility' and 'friendships of pleasure'. A 'friendship of utility' is one in which the relationship is maintained because it is in some way useful to both parties. One example of this kind of relationship would be a 'friendship' between two business associates which is maintained because it is useful for their respective business interests. This type of friendship is based primarily in self-interest and, as Aristotle (2000: 146) puts it, each person does not love the other person in their own right 'but only in so far as they will obtain some good for themselves from him [sic].' A 'friendship of pleasure' is, by contrast, one in which people maintain the relationship because they find each others' company enjoyable or because they enjoy doing certain activities together. Whilst this type of relationship is not so blatantly instrumental as a 'friendship of utility', it is still a more superficial kind of friendship. For in a 'friendship of pleasure', each person values the other not because of who they fundamentally are as a person, but because there is one aspect of them that they enjoy or find pleasant (for example, their taste, sense of humour, choice of leisure interests, etc.).

Aristotle saw these two types of friendship as being inferior for two reasons. First, one can engage in either of these kinds of friendship and still be a bad person. For example, a businessman might be selfish, unkind or unfaithful, but as long as these qualities did not harm the business interests of his associate, a successful 'friendship of utility' could still be maintained between them. Similarly, a woman might enjoy playing tennis with her friend, regardless of the fact that her friend might be greedy or insensitive, as long as her friend's bad traits did not spoil their enjoyment of the game together. Second, Aristotle saw these types of friendship as inferior because they tended to be short-lived. A 'friendship of utility' will be maintained only as long as it has some use for both parties. If one of the businessmen loses his job, the other will probably lose contact with him because there is nothing to be gained from maintaining it. Similarly a 'friendship of pleasure' will tend to last only as long as each person finds the other's company enjoyable. If one of the tennis players gets injured or decides that she does not enjoy tennis any more, then the other will not maintain contact with her unless there is some other activity that they enjoy together. Aristotle did not deny that 'friendships of utility' or 'friendships of pleasure' had their value and role in society. After all, it is important for us to spend time with people who can help us in some way or whose company we enjoy. Nevertheless, Aristotle argued that whilst these types of friendship might be necessary, there was another kind of friendship that was better than either of them.

The ideal friendship that Aristotle identified was a 'friendship of virtue'. He defined this kind of relationship in the following way:

> Those who wish good things to a friend *for his own sake* [emphasis added] are friends most of all, since they are disposed in this way towards each other because of what they are, not for any incidental reason. (Aristotle, 2000: 147)

A 'friendship of virtue' is thus a deeper form of relationship in which each person has a fundamental love and regard for the other. The friendship itself arises out of this fundamental love and regard, rather than simply out of mutual benefit or enjoyment (though a 'friendship of virtue' will, at least for some of the time, have useful or enjoyable parts to it). A number of other brief comments can also be made about this type of ideal friendship. First, whilst people who engage in a 'friendship of virtue' are unlikely to lose all self-interest, they are primarily motivated in that friendship by a loving regard for the other. Second, the love and regard in the friendship are based on a *mutual* understanding and respect. If one person demonstrates a fundamental regard for the other, but the other person does not reciprocate, then this clearly falls short of the ideal. Third, it is only possible for people of good character to build and experience this kind of friendship. We noted before that bad moral traits do not necessarily prevent people from experiencing friendships of utility or pleasure, but if someone is cruel, selfish or greedy then they will find it much harder to sustain the depth of regard and understanding necessary for a more profound friendship. Finally, to develop such a friendship is a slow process. For to develop a true understanding and regard for another person requires 'time and familiarity', as Aristotle comments:

> [People] cannot know each other until they have eaten... together; nor can they accept each other or be friends until each has shown himself to be worthy of love and gained the other's confidence.... For though the wish to friendship arises quickly, friendship does not.' (Aristotle, 2000: 147)

Aristotle's notion of the ideal friendship may not seem particularly startling to us as contemporary Western culture is steeped in the Romantic belief that an intimate, loving relationship with another person is integral to our well-being. What can seem more alien in Aristotle's thought is his understanding of how friendship is modified by social roles and hierarchies. In this context, it is important to recognise that Aristotle had a far more hierarchical view of society (in which the aristocracy were, for example, more important than the masses, and men were more important than women) than we do in our more egalitarian societies. For Aristotle, such social hierarchies had important implications for friendship. For example, if the social divide was too great between two people then he believed that friendship between them was not possible. Furthermore, in instances where one friend had a higher social status than another, Aristotle (2000: 152) claimed that the affection between them should be 'proportional' to their status. In other words, the more social status a person had, the more affection they deserved from their friends. Whilst these elitist assumptions will seem alien to many people in Western society today, there is one element of Aristotle's thought on friendship and social roles that can still be helpful for us. Although Aristotle did believe that an ideal friendship can only exist between people who are social equals, he also recognised that genuine friendship could take place across social roles and classes. In such friendships, Aristotle (2000: 163) suggested that both parties could give, as well as gain, something important from the friendship, but that the nature of what was given or received might be different for each person. Thus, Aristotle suggested, a wealthy man might demonstrate friendship through his material support of a poorer friend, and this friend might demonstrate his friendship through explicit displays of honour and respect towards the richer friend. Again we might feel somewhat uncomfortable about the hierarchical assumptions in Aristotle's thought here, but there is a useful underlying point about friendship and social roles to which we will return shortly.

Throughout this book we have been thinking about pastoral work as religiously motivated practice that seeks to enable people to have a greater experience of the good life. If we accept Aristotle's notion that a particular kind of friendship is an integral part of the good life, then is it possible for the pastoral relationship itself to demonstrate certain qualities of a 'friendship of virtue'? In other words, is it possible for people to have a greater experience of the good life, not simply as a consequence of the pastoral worker's actions or of the content of a pastoral conversation, but through the very interpersonal qualities of the pastoral relationship itself? Exploring the relevance of Aristotle's understanding of friendship for the pastoral relationship will be the focus of the remainder of this chapter.

Pastoral Practice and 'Moderated' Friendship

There are two ways in which I believe Aristotle's notion of friendship offers helpful insights for understanding important qualities of the pastoral relationship. First, if pastoral care is to avoid an arid professionalism, it may be argued that it needs to involve an emphasis upon love, as well as an understanding of clear professional boundaries. As Bennett Moore (2001: 3) suggests, the very term *pastoral* is 'centrally focused on the practices of loving concern.' To say that the pastoral relationship needs to be a loving one, however, begs the question about what understanding of love we have in mind when we say this. As we have seen, Aristotle identifies ideal qualities of human relating as being a fundamental regard for another individual based on a clear understanding of who they are as a person. This attitude is different to a universal 'unconditional positive regard' or a generalised 'love for humanity'. For rather than being a generalised attitude towards all people, Aristotle's 'friendship of virtue' involves a specific love for another person that has built up over time as one's knowledge of them grows and deepens. If the pastoral relationship is to follow the form of a 'friendship of virtue', then the partners in this relationship need to have spent time and energy together in building a relationship in which love and understanding is possible. If we follow Aristotle's thought at this point, then, the 'loving concern' of pastoral practice is not a vague aspiration, but a hard-won love of a specific person in a specific time and place.

Aristotle's notion of a 'friendship of virtue' can thus help us to focus on the importance of love and understanding for specific individuals within pastoral relationships. Is it reasonable to suggest, however, that the pastoral relationship should be like a 'friendship of virtue' between two equal partners? In the previous chapter I suggested that it was inappropriate to think of a pastoral relationship as a friendship. If we return to thinking about issues of power and boundaries in the pastoral relationship, it is clear that the pastoral worker and those for whom they care are not equals in terms of their social roles, power and responsibilities.

Pastoral workers usually hold more institutional power than those for whom they care, and pastoral workers cannot expect to receive the same degree of emotional and spiritual support in return from those for whom they care. To distinguish between the social roles of the pastoral carer and the pastoral care-seeker is not to imply that one is more valuable than the other, but does indicate that the pastoral worker typically holds greater power and particular responsibilities in the context of this relationship. A pastoral relationship is therefore different to an equal friendship in which neither person has particular institutional power or responsibilities that influence that relationship.

Is the concept of a 'friendship of virtue' really applicable to a pastoral relationship then? It is here that Aristotle's thought makes a second useful contribution in terms of his recognition of the effects of differences in social role and status upon friendships. Again, whilst we may not warm to his elitist view of society, Aristotle is helpful in clarifying that a friendship between equals is different to a friendship between two people in which there is some difference in their social roles, power and responsibilities. Following this point, we might say that a pastoral relationship cannot be a friendship between equals, but can be a friendship based on social difference. Or to adapt the work of Alastair Campbell (1984) on love and professional care, we might describe the pastoral relationship as a 'moderated friendship.'

A 'moderated friendship' is one in which mutual regard is still present, but in which what each person gives and receives in the relationship may be different. The pastoral worker therefore gives emotional, practical and spiritual support to those for whom they care, in a way that they would not normally expect to receive in return from them. A person receiving pastoral care can demonstrate regard for the pastoral carer through valuing the carer's individuality and through a willingness not to make unreasonable or abusive demands upon the carer's energy. A pastoral relationship thus functions as a 'moderated friendship' when it involves both a mutual regard between carer and care-seeker and the maintenance of appropriate boundaries within the relationship.

Understanding the pastoral relationship in these terms gives rise to a number of wider implications. For example, we noted earlier the idea that a 'friendship of virtue' could only be built and sustained if those involved in this relationship were of good character. Unlike 'friendships of utility' and 'friendships of pleasure' which can be maintained between people of bad character, qualities such as greed, selfishness and indifference would undermine a deeper 'friendship of virtue'. If we understand some moderated form of a 'friendship of virtue' as an ideal for the pastoral relationship, then this raises questions about what moral qualities the participants in the pastoral relationship need to bring to it. Rather than being a purely technical, therapeutic relationship, the pastoral encounter therefore rests on the capacity for pastoral carers to demonstrate virtues such as love, faithfulness, respect and patience. Thinking about the pastoral relationship in terms of a 'friendship of virtue', however, does not simply highlight the importance of the virtues that the pastoral carer brings to the relationship, but also raises the issue of the way that the person receiving care relates to the pastoral worker. Again we noted earlier that a 'friendship of virtue' is a mutual relationship between two people in which both demonstrate an attitude of regard towards the other. If a 'friendship of virtue' is indeed a model for a good pastoral relationship then this suggests that a person receiving pastoral care also has responsibilities to give due regard to the pastoral worker. If a pastoral worker finds that they are abused or exploited in a pastoral relationship then this relationship is failing to give either the pastoral carer or careseeker a greater experience of the good life. In the face of such exploitation, some form of action is appropriate to move the pastoral relationship on to a more healthy, or at least less damaging, basis. Recognising this point is important in religious environments in which the idealisation of self-sacrifice can make it harder for pastoral workers to think about what expectations, demands or attitudes from care-seekers are unreasonable, excessive or unhealthy (see Boyd & Lynch, 1999).

Thinking about pastoral relationships in terms of 'friendships of virtue' also raises the issue of time in the pastoral relationship. If, as Aristotle claimed, the best kind of friendship can only emerge over an extended period of time, then the quality of the pastoral relationship is likely, in part, to be influenced by how much time the pastoral carer and careseeker have been able to spend in getting to know each other better. This is not to suggest that short-term pastoral encounters are not of value. Indeed for pastoral practitioners working, for example, in hospital chaplaincies, much of their work is likely to consist of offering valuable emotional support and containment to people whom they might only meet on one or two occasions. Similarly short-term pastoral counselling relationships can also be of genuine value to clients who are experiencing particular crises (see, for examples, Childs, 1990). It remains true, though, that in longer-term pastoral relationships a quality of understanding and regard may develop which is harder to develop in briefer contacts. This degree of understanding may be particularly important when the pastoral carer and care-seeker come to discuss a moral dilemma that the care-seeker may be facing, and we shall return to this point in more detail in the following chapter.

Summary

In this book as a whole, then, we have been exploring different dimensions of the pastoral encounter that influence the care-seeker's ability to experience something more of the good life. In this chapter, we have explored the idea that, in addition to appropriate boundaries, pastoral relationships will lead to a greater experience of the good life if they demonstrate the kind of interpersonal qualities that Aristotle observed in 'friendships of virtue.' Moral reflection on the practice of pastoral care thus needs to engage not only with questions of the social and cultural context of that care and the appropriate boundaries of pastoral care, but also with questions of what kinds of interpersonal relationships help to further human well-being. Thinking morally about these different aspects of the pastoral encounter will generate a far richer understanding of pastoral work and provide an important context for the pressing issue of how pastoral practitioners seek to work with moral dilemmas faced by those who seek their help. It is to this issue that we will turn in the next chapter.

Notes

1   For a fuller discussion of classical ideas of friendship, see, for example, Price, 1989.

7

Exploring ethical dilemmas in the pastoral conversation

So far, then, we have thought about three different dimensions of the pastoral encounter that invite moral reflection: the social context of the pastoral encounter, the boundaries of the pastoral encounter and the interpersonal qualities of the pastoral relationship. In this chapter we will turn our attention to the area that is perhaps most commonly seen as the point where ethics becomes relevant to pastoral practice, namely the exploration of moral dilemmas in the pastoral conversation.

Within this chapter we will briefly explore different styles of ethical thinking that can shape the way in which pastoral practitioners perceive and respond to moral dilemmas. We will then go on to explore frameworks that can help pastoral workers to develop their capacity for practical moral reflection, before discussing briefly the issue of ethical confrontation within the pastoral conversation.

We will begin with a case study that will provide a focus for our discussion:

Sarah is an ordained minister working in a local parish church in a suburb of a major city. One of her parishioners, Paul, makes an appointment to see her. Paul is a single man, in his late 20s, who is a committed and popular member of her congregation. He is involved in a range of activities within the church, including helping to lead the church youth group and occasionally preaching at church services.

At this meeting Paul explains to Sarah that over a long period of time he has come to realise that he is gay. This has been a difficult and lonely process for him, but through it he has been forced to recognise that he is only sexually attracted to men and that the kind of romantic relationship he would like to develop would be with another man. Over the past year, he has begun to develop friendships with other gay men in the area. There is one friend, Nick, with whom Paul has become particularly close, to the point where they now both feel that they are in love with each other. Nick would like to start a sexual relationship with Paul, and Paul feels that he would also like this but is unsure about whether he can reconcile having a gay sexual relationship (even if a committed one) with his Christian convictions. Paul asks Sarah what she thinks he should do in this situation.

Again, you might want to take a moment to pause and reflect on how you might respond to Paul in this situation. What would be your initial reaction? What further questions might you want to ask him, and what kind of response would you want to make to him?

The way in which we respond to Paul's dilemma will reflect our own style of ethical thinking. By 'style' of ethical thinking, I mean not only our belief about what is generally right and wrong, but also the way that we go about working out what right and wrong means in a particular situation. Across the (recent) history of moral philosophy and theological ethics there have been two opposing major styles of ethical thinking, and these different styles are often evident in the way in which individuals think about moral dilemmas.

One of these major styles of ethical reflection has been called the *deontological* approach. 'Deontology' literally means the study of what it is necessary to do, or the study of duty. With its emphasis on duty, the deontological approach is therefore focused on what moral rules or ethical responsibilities we need to fulfil in the particular situations that we find ourselves in. Typically, ethical thinkers who use a deontological approach have tried to identify universal moral laws that everyone (in all places and at all times) should follow. Immanuel Kant, one of the key thinkers in the deontological tradition, thus argued that one of the principles on which we should judge whether an action was moral or not was to 'act as if the maxim of your action was to become through your will a universal law of nature' (Vardy & Grosch, 1994: 69). In other words, Kant was suggesting that we should judge what constitutes a moral act on the basis of whether it reflects a moral law which we believe should be universally binding on all people. Deontological ethics are therefore rule-based, and this approach assumes that we fulfil our moral duty if we keep whatever moral rules are relevant to the circumstances in which we find ourselves.

An important issue upon which individuals adopting a deontological approach have disagreed is how one decides what constitutes a moral law (see Frankena, 1973). Kant argued that it was possible to identify these moral rules through rational reflection. Others have suggested that human reason is flawed, however, and that our knowledge of the absolute moral law is only possible through divine revelation (for example, the giving of the Ten Commandments). This approach has been described as 'divine-command' deontology. A further approach is to see our understanding of moral laws as arising neither from conscious, rational reflection, nor from the voice of God, but from our intuitive knowledge of what is right and wrong.

As well as disagreeing on how to identify universal moral laws, deontological ethicists may also come to quite different conclusions when thinking about the same moral dilemma. In thinking about whether one should be a vegetarian or not, for example, a Kantian deontological ethicist might argue that there are no rational grounds to insist that everyone should be vegetarians, whilst a divine-command deontologist might argue on the basis of their religious tradition that eating meat is specifically forbidden. Or equally, a rational argument could be made for why all people should be vegetarians, whilst a religious tradition could be seen to permit the eating of meat. What deontological ethicists have in common, then, is not the particular ethical conclusions that they reach, but a basic commitment to identifying universal moral laws and to upholding these in a consistent way.

It is possible to see how some pastoral workers would approach Paul's case using a predominantly deontological style of ethical thinking. For such pastoral workers, a key issue that would shape their response to Paul would be whether entering a gay sexual relationship breaks any universal moral laws or not. Pastoral practitioners holding conservative Christian moral beliefs will tend to interpret Paul's dilemma in the light of their belief that God, through Scripture, has prohibited gay sexual relationships (see, for example, Green and Holloway, 1980; Stott, 1990). Such a 'divine-command' deontological perspective will inevitably lead the pastoral worker to think that a good outcome in Paul's situation would be for him to maintain a celibate lifestyle. Equally, though, it would be possible for a pastoral worker to take a deontological approach to Paul's dilemma and believe that it would be acceptable for him to pursue a sexual relationship with Nick. For if the pastoral worker believed that such a sexual relationship did not contravene any moral law, then there would be no grounds for objecting to it (see, for example, Countryman, 1989). For pastoral workers adopting a deontological style of ethical thinking, though, a common concern would be to identify any moral laws that were relevant to Paul's situation (particularly in relation to the expression of gay sexuality) and to hope that Paul would fulfil his moral duty in observing these.

The emphasis within a deontological approach to ethics on the consistent adherence to moral rules has a certain clarity to it – particularly when one has established which moral rules it is essential to follow. This consistency and clarity, however, is the basis of some criticism of the deontological approach. Imagine, for example, that a person is living in Nazi Germany and harbouring Jews in their house. A group of Nazi soldiers comes to their house and asks if they are hiding any Jews there. If that person maintained a deontological emphasis on consistently following moral rules, and believed that an essential moral rule was never to tell lies, then they would be morally compelled to admit that there were Jews hiding in the house. In this situation, following a moral rule could actually lead to a greater evil taking place.

This objection to a deontological approach to ethics reflects basic assumptions of a second major style of ethical thought, the *consequentialist* approach. As its name suggests, a consequentialist approach to ethics is concerned with what consequences follow a particular action. In this view, an action is morally good if it leads to positive outcomes and wrong if it leads to damaging or harmful consequences. One writer who has been an important exponent of this approach in theological circles has been Joseph Fletcher who wrote a book titled *Situation Ethics* (Fletcher, 1966). Fletcher argued that the deontological approach's search for universal laws was ultimately flawed because no moral law could ever be sufficiently sensitive to the complexities of real human situations. Indeed Fletcher produced a series of case examples in which the breaking of moral laws, such as do not kill or do not commit adultery, actually led to a greater good (such as communities being saved from destruction or families being reunited) that would not have been achieved if the laws had been rigidly adhered to. Using the language of earlier utilitarian thinkers, Fletcher argued that we should make our moral decisions on the basis of an 'agapeic calculus'. In other words, we should make a judgment in each moral dilemma that we face as to what action would produce the most loving and constructive consequences possible to those involved.

As with the deontological approach, the consequentialist style of thinking has much room for disagreement within it. One of the key issues here is how one defines 'good outcomes'. Is a good outcome one that produces the greatest amount of pleasure for those involved, or should some other trait or quality be pursued above pleasure, such as love or integrity? This leads us back to our discussion in Chapters 1 and 3 about how we should define the good life. For consequentialists to argue that actions are morally good when they produce good consequences is again clear enough, but does beg the question of what we mean by 'good'.

In terms of Paul's dilemma, then, a pastoral worker adopting a consequentialist response would think not in terms of moral rules applicable to his situation, but about the consequences of him entering a sexual relationship with Nick. If the pastoral worker felt that Paul had not fully thought through the implications of entering this relationship, or was not emotionally ready for it, then they might see the effects of a sexual relationship between Paul and Nick as potentially negative. If entering this relationship would be likely to be emotionally damaging for Paul,

Nick, or both of them, then a consequentialist perspective would tend to see this as a bad course of action to take. Alternatively, though, if a pastoral worker thinking along consequentialist lines believed that the positive outcomes of this relationship (for example, in terms of greater self-expression and intimacy for Paul and Nick) outweighed any negative consequences, then they would see it as a good thing for Paul to enter into it.

Just as the deontological approach to ethical reflection has been subject to criticism, so important questions have also been raised about the consequentialist approach. One criticism is that a consequentialist approach rests on the assumption that it is possible to predict with some certainty what the consequences of human acts will be. Yet often, given the complexities of human existence, it is actually very difficult to make such predictions with any certainty. Furthermore, the question can also be raised whether an act can be seen as good if it produces a considerable benefit to many people whilst being profoundly damaging to a smaller group? This opens up the question as to whether all people (or indeed all sentient beings) have basic rights that should not be infringed even if there is a considerable benefit to others from doing so.

Identifying the deontological and consequentialist styles of ethical thinking can be helpful in terms of making us more aware of some of the ways we ourselves tend to approach thinking about moral dilemmas. In practice, it is unlikely (unless we live our lives as trained moral philosophers) that we are entirely consistent in our styles of ethical thinking. Sometimes when we face moral dilemmas we are concerned with rules and at other times with consequences of actions. Certainly when I have explored Paul's scenario with students in an ethics class, I have found that some people object to Paul entering a sexual relationship on both deontological and consequentialist grounds at the same time. They argue that Paul should not begin a sexual relationship with Nick partly because the Bible prohibits homosexual relationships and partly because it would lead to bad emotional and spiritual consequences for him. Equally, other students have argued that Paul should pursue this sexual relationship because the Bible should not be read as prohibiting it and the consequences of this relationship could be very positive. Our styles of moral reflection and moral argument can therefore be inconsistent and focused more on trying to demonstrate the rightness of our own prior moral beliefs. Thinking about the deontological and consequentialist styles of ethical reflection can help us to become more aware of situations where our moral thinking is inconsistent, however, and this can at least open up the possibility of new ways of thinking about dilemmas that we face.

Developing Practical Moral Reflection

Moral philosophers and theological ethicists have often worked on the basis of trying to argue which method of moral reflection (whether deontological, consequentialist or other) is most likely to enable us to make correct moral decisions. Unless they have a particular interest in ethical theory, however, pastoral practitioners may adopt a more pragmatic approach and see such methods of moral reflection more as tools that can help us to explore different dimensions of ethical dilemmas. Moral philosophers and theological ethicists thus often appear to begin from the perspective of a theoretical framework which they then apply to ethical problems. Pastoral practitioners, on the other hand, find themselves confronted by such dilemmas in their day-to-day work and then seek to make use of whatever tools can help their moral reflection.

Thinking about different styles of ethical thinking (such as the deontological and consequentialist approaches) is one way of developing different perspectives on a moral dilemma. Another is to develop a more general framework of questions that we may wish to explore when we face an ethically-complex situation. Earlier in Chapter 3, we noted Don Browning's notion of different levels of practical moral reflection. Using Browning's model can indeed help to identify different levels of issues involved in the moral dilemmas we face. It has been argued that although comprehensive, Browning's model may be too complex for individual pastoral workers to use, either in specific pastoral conversations or in subsequent supervision of their pastoral practice (Pattison, 1988: 45).

An alternative framework for practical moral reflection that draws on much that is valuable in Browning's work, but that some pastoral workers may find more accessible, has been created by Rebekah Miles (see Miles, 1999: 27–34). Miles suggests that when thinking about ethical dilemmas, pastoral practitioners may find it useful to have four central questions in mind:

1. *What is happening?* This question invites a close analysis of the moral dilemma that is being faced. Who is involved in this dilemma? What do we know about them? What important qualities, motivations and needs do they bring to this situation? What significant dynamics influence the interaction of those involved in this dilemma? What has led to this dilemma arising? By developing this kind of situational analysis, a pastoral practitioner may be able to be more sensitive to the nature of the particular dilemma that they are facing, rather than assuming that it is simply an example

of a general moral dilemma that can be responded to in a textbook fashion.

2. *Who are we and where are we going?* These linked questions invite the pastoral practitioner to compare their analysis of the dynamics of the specific moral dilemma with a more general understanding of the human condition and the purpose of human existence. The way in which we perceive particular moral problems will be influenced by our understanding of what it means to be human, both in terms of essential human needs and qualities and in terms of what we should aspire to be as human persons. The process of comparing the specific analysis of the moral dilemma with these more general ideas can help us to consider what kinds of resolutions to this dilemma might be more likely to promote the basic humanity of those involved within it. This process thus has a consequentialist ethos underlying it.

3. *What rules and principles do we follow and how do we make exceptions?* If we assume that the moral traditions developed within religious communities over many centuries have some validity to them, then it will be important to ask if there are any rules or principles within that tradition that are especially relevant to the particular dilemma that we face. In raising this question it is important both to allow the moral wisdom that may lie behind such rules and principles to speak to our situation, but also to be sensitive to where those rules and principles may not be wholly applicable. Miles comments that the Christian presumption against divorce may be an important principle to bring to crises in particular marriages, but that the pastoral practitioner should also be open to the possibility of divorce being the best option in exceptional circumstances. This line of reflection clearly has more of a deontological emphasis within it.

4. *Who is God and what difference does it make?* Miles observes that moral reflection for pastoral workers will ultimately return them to basic theological questions. What is the nature of God, and how should we understand ourselves and the world in the light of who or what God is? For example if we emphasise God as Creator, how might our understanding of the goodness and integrity of creation influence our understanding of the specific dilemma that we face? Or if we perceive God as judge, then what responses to the dilemma would be more likely to provoke divine judgment? What

images or metaphors of God should also be balanced against each other in our thinking in order to allow for a richer and more-balanced moral decision?

Miles' framework for practical moral thinking has much to commend it in terms of its clarity and flexibility. Returning to our original case example of Paul's dilemma about entering a gay relationship, we can see how Miles' framework would raise a number of important questions that would help us to develop our reflection on this situation. For example:

1. *What is happening?* What do we know about Paul and Nick as people? What do we know about the wider network of friends and wider communities that they are a part of? What strengths, limitations and vulnerabilities do Paul and Nick bring to this situation? What is Paul's understanding of his sexuality and what do we know about how this understanding has emerged?
2. *Who are we and where are we going?* What is the proper nature and function of human sexuality? Can healthy sexual relationships only take one form (for example, heterosexual relationships in the context of marriage) or can they take a wider range of forms? To what extent are the needs for intimacy and sexual expression integral to a full human existence? In what circumstances is celibacy an integral part of human well-being?
3. *What rules and principles do we follow and how do we make exceptions?* What moral rules might be relevant to Paul's situation? Given his commitment to the Christian tradition, does this tradition rule against any form of gay sexual relationship? Can meaningful moral rules about contemporary gay sexuality be drawn from the text of the Bible or from the Church's wider tradition? Are rules that may be evident in the text of the Bible (for example, in the 'Holiness Code' in the book of Leviticus) really applicable to our current, very different, cultural circumstances? Even if, from a Christian perspective, it is possible to establish a valid moral rule against gay sexual relationships, is this rule applicable in Paul's case? Would a rigid adherence to a traditional Christian moral rule be more harmful than helpful in Paul's case?

4. *Who is God and what differences does it make?* What concepts or metaphors of God shape the way in which we interpret and respond to Paul's situation? If we see God primarily as King and Judge, in what way might this lead to a different interpretation of Paul's case than if we see God as Love or as Friend (see McFague, 1987)? What is Paul's understanding of God and how does this relate to his experience of his sexuality? In what ways can Paul be supported in developing both notions of God and understandings of his sexuality that are healthy and constructive?

Ultimately a framework such as this one developed by Miles serves primarily to generate further questions that we need to think about. Having these questions raised is important, however, in helping us to think about moral dilemmas in more thorough and critical ways. Answering these questions will require hard work on our part that draws on our own personal experience, the moral wisdom of the communities that we belong to, and our own lived spirituality. In addition to these there is also value in wider academic and theoretical resources that help us to think about our images of God, the hermeneutical issues of using religious texts in moral reflection, methods of moral reflection and the nature of a good and authentic human existence. A brief summary of academic texts that may be useful for exploring these issues further is given towards the end of this book.

Ethical Confrontation in the Pastoral Conversation

If the pastoral conversation is an important place for the discussion and exploration of moral dilemmas, then this begs a question that was raised back in the first chapter of this book. Is the function of the pastoral conversation simply to reinforce the values held by the client and to support the client in whatever moral choices they make? Or does the pastoral worker have some particular role in bringing their own values to bear on the discussion of the moral dilemmas that their clients face? If the pastoral worker brings their own values into the discussion of client's moral dilemmas, does this not run the risk of becoming a damagingly judgmental and moralistic approach to pastoral practice?

John Hoffman, in his detailed discussion of ethical confrontation in the context of the therapeutic relationship, makes the following point:

... the reluctance to issue a moral challenge in therapy reflects in part a growing disillusionment in modern society with all authority, as well as the insertion of a covert morality under the guise of psychologically founded fact. But I have argued that human existence always has a moral dimension, a reality made only more urgent by the significant ethical aspects in the major social crises of our time. Any therapy ... which seeks on these or any other grounds to avoid a true ethical witness is bound to be inadequate because of its failure to equip counsellees to function in the real world, a world of moral choices. Moral confrontation in therapy is thus an ethical necessity. (Hoffman, 1979: 78)

Despite being written more than twenty years ago, Hoffman's comment remains topical. Contemporary society has typically tended to emphasise the right of the individual, within certain limits, to define truth as they themselves wish (see Bruce, 1995). Pastoral workers (and other professional carers) can therefore be reluctant to bring their own values explicitly into their therapeutic conversations for fear of undermining their clients' autonomy. Yet, as we argued in the opening chapter of this book, value-free pastoral practice is not possible. Thus, Hoffman argues, rather than allowing a set of values covertly to influence our therapeutic practice, it is better, where appropriate, for these values to be explicit so that clients can be helped to engage with the complex task of making moral choices in the postmodern world.

This process of thinking in a challenging way about clients' values and moral decisions does not necessarily imply that the pastoral worker is trying to 'make' the client more 'moral' in their outlook on life. Indeed much of this challenge may be about raising questions about values that the client holds that are in fact unnecessarily punitive and life-denying. Ethical confrontation, in the instance of the case of Paul's thoughts about entering a gay sexual relationship, could therefore be about challenging negative moral views about homosexuality that he might hold, which are out of keeping with the Christian celebration of love and intimate human relationship.

So how can the pastoral worker's own values or moral reflections be brought into the pastoral conversation in a way that is not abusive or damaging to the client? It is here, I would suggest, that the quality of the pastoral relationship is crucial. In the previous chapter, I suggested that a pastoral encounter will promote the client's experience of the good life if that encounter contains elements of the Aristotelian 'friendship of virtue'. If the pastoral relationship is therefore one in which mutual regard and understanding are present then the experience of the relationship itself is a beneficial thing to both participants. Not only this, though, but such a pastoral relationship is an important context in which open and honest moral discussion of issues facing the client becomes possible. Earlier in this chapter, we noted that an important part of Miles' framework for practical moral reflection on ethical dilemmas was a good understanding of those involved within it. Such understanding only really becomes possible when we have been able to spend time with a person, learning about their experiences, motivations, anxieties and commitments. It is when we know a person well that we are more able to raise questions about the moral decisions that they are making or the values that are influencing them.

Engaging in open, honest and potentially challenging moral reflection with clients is therefore less likely to be damaging if it takes place in the context of an established pastoral relationship characterised by mutual empathy and regard. Difficult questions arise, however, for pastoral workers who may be faced with conversations about moral dilemmas with people about whom they know very little. A hospital chaplain may, for example, be approached by someone they have not met before to discuss whether or not it would be morally right for that person to terminate their pregnancy. In such instances the pastoral worker can face a difficult tension between maintaining their own ethical integrity (by not simply uncritically supporting the client's moral choice) and conducting the pastoral conversation in a sensitive and helpful manner. Certainly for the pastoral practitioner to introduce their own values into a conversation is something that needs to be done with great caution if they understand little about the psychological, spiritual or moral background of the person to whom they are talking. Any open discussion of moral issues facing the client would need to be conducted carefully and in the context of a conversation in which empathy and fundamental acceptance are conveyed to the client. Without such a safe relational framework, any moral stance taken by the pastoral practitioner risks being experienced as judgmental, moralistic and irrelevant by the client.

From 'Moral Decisions' to 'Moral Character'

The final area to be explored in this chapter is to attempt to place the very notion of 'moral dilemmas' in a wider context. So far, our discussion in this chapter has tended to assume that individuals and groups can experience situations that represent 'moral dilemmas' and that through careful reflection it may be possible to identify better ways of responding to those dilemmas. Indeed the deontological and consequentialist styles of ethical thinking can be seen as different ways of approaching moral dilemmas in a thoughtful and reflective way.

Whilst reflection is an important part of the process of responding to moral issues, an emphasis on reflection alone runs the risk of neglecting other parts of who we are as human beings that influence our moral decisions. It is here that a third major tradition of ethical thinking, 'virtue ethics', has a particularly significant contribution to make. 'Virtue ethics' is an approach to ethics that sees the moral character of the individual as a crucial resource for their ability to act in morally good ways (see MacIntyre, 1985). Thus the 'virtues' that a person has developed will be profoundly significant in shaping the way in which they characteristically respond to situations in which they find themselves. This concept is neatly illustrated in the following story told by the 'virtue ethicist', Stanley Hauerwas:

> I have a friend who travels a great deal. Anyone who travels knows that there is something inherently tempting about getting on airplanes and going places where you are not well known. The experience conveys a freedom that might allow a casual sexual engagement where no strings are attached or any consequences ever follow. My friend, who confesses he often enjoys fantasising in such a manner, was once taken aback while he was on an almost empty flight returning home and a stewardess actually proposed that they might enjoy one another's company for a while. My friend candidly admits that the first thing that occurred to him was not the rule 'Thou shalt not commit adultery' but, 'How could I explain to my wife why I was late?' But that question was enough for him to refuse the offer, because it occurred to him he would have to lie, and while he might even have thought up a good lie, he simply did not want to begin that kind of life.
>   That lie … would have changed who he was. In refusing the stewardess he did not feel as if he had made a 'decision'; the decision had already been made by the kind of person he was and the kind of life he had with his family. Indeed, all the 'decision' did was make him aware of what he already was, since he really did not know that he had developed the habit of faithfulness. (Hauerwas, 1983: 129–30).

Hauerwas' story clearly illustrates the idea that, as moral agents, we do not simply make rational decisions based on our judgments of the particular circumstances in which we find ourselves, but that we are people whose character will shape what decisions we can even contemplate thinking about. From a 'virtue ethics' perspective, therefore, seeing ethics simply as a series of isolated decisions that we make when we encounter situations that we experience as 'moral dilemmas' is to miss the point. Rather, ethics concern a wider set of questions about what kinds of virtues we need to develop in order to live moral lives and what we need to do in order to nurture and maintain those virtues. This raises questions about what resources (for example, stories, symbols, rituals) and what kinds of relationships help us to form good moral characters that enable us to engage virtuously with life (see Hauerwas, 1981).

Summary

In this chapter we have explored some specific issues that relate to how we think about and disuss moral dilemmas. Throughout the book as a whole though, we have seen that moral reflection is relevant for pastoral practice, not only when we are confronted with ethical dilemmas. Rather, thinking morally about pastoral practice means thinking more broadly about the nature of the good life, and the nature of the resources and relationships that we need to enable us to live moral lives.

As I suggested in the Introduction, it may not be realistic to imagine that we can achieve final or definitive answers to the questions raised in this book. Nevertheless, through thinking about these issues, we can begin to articulate clearly the values about which we care deeply. If we can understand and express these values, whilst being open to critical questions that others may raise about them, we may develop greater thoughtfulness and integrity in our pastoral practice. Ultimately our hope must be that this process of moral refection is one that can lead us slowly to a clearer understanding of what is good and valuable in life and towards practice that genuinely promotes human well-being.

Further Reading

Whilst I have tried to be fairly comprehensive in the questions and issues that I have explored in this book, I am aware that my approach here raises as many (if not more) questions than I have answered. It will be useful for me to give some idea of other texts that might be helpful for further reading in this area as you continue to think about these questions. The books listed below merely represent an illustrative list – there are many other books that you will be able to find that will help you think more about your particular interests and concerns. You may also find yourself disagreeing with the methods of moral reflection or ethical conclusions that some of the following writers adopt. Such disagreement, though, can be actually quite helpful to the process of developing your own style of moral thinking. The following is therefore offered in the spirit of some initial suggestions that might form the basis of your own developing, reading and searching.

Introductory Books

A number of books have been written that offer some initial introduction to the field of ethics. Some of these approach the subject from the perspective of moral philosophy, and useful examples of these are:

Frankena, W. (1973) *Ethics* (2nd edition). Englewood Cliffs, NJ: Prentice-Hall.
Gensler, H. (1998) *Ethics: A Contemporary Introduction*. London: Routledge.
Singer, P. (ed.) (1993) *A Companion to Ethics*. Oxford: Blackwell.

Other books offer useful historical overviews of the development of moral thinking, such as:

Arrington, R. (1998) *Western Ethics: An Historical Introduction*. Oxford: Blackwell.
MacIntyre, A. (1993) *A Short History of Ethics*. London: Routledge.

In addition to more general books on moral philosophy, a number of introductory books provide helpful resources for thinking about the relationship between theology, religious belief and ethics. Examples of these are:

Boulton, W. et al (eds) (1994) *From Christ to the World: Introductory Readings in Christian Ethics*. Grand Rapids, Mich.: Eerdmans.

Hoose, B. (ed.) (1998) *Christian Ethics: An Introduction*. London: Cassell.

Sherwin, B. (2000) *Jewish Ethics for the Twenty-First Century*. Syracuse, NY: Syracuse University Press.

Vardy, P. & Grosch, P. (1994) *The Puzzle of Ethics*. London: Fount.

Specific Themes/Issues

As well as introductory books on ethics, there is also a very extensive selection of books available that explore particular themes and issues in ethics. Books that may be particularly relevant for pastoral workers are:

Beauchamp, T. and Childress, J. (1994) *Principles of Biomedical Ethics*, Oxford: Oxford University Press.

Bond, T. (2000) *Standards and Ethics for Counselling in Action* (2nd edition). London: Sage.

The series of books on 'New Studies in Christian Ethics' published by the Cambridge University Press is also a useful resource, with particularly relevant titles being:

Gill, R. (1999) *Churchgoing and Christian Ethics*. Cambridge: Cambridge University Press.

Northcott, M. (1996) *The Environment and Christian Ethics*. Cambridge: Cambridge University Press.

Parsons, S. (1996) *Feminism and Christian Ethics*. Cambridge: Cambridge University Press.

As noted earlier in this book, it is helpful to be aware of values and styles of ethical thinking beyond our immediate cultural context. Books that can help to develop this cross-cultural moral awareness are:

Tiles, J. (2000) *Moral Measures: An Introduction to Ethics East and West*. London: Routledge.

Wentzel Wolfe, R. & Gudorf, C. (eds) (1999) *Ethics and World Religions: Cross-Cultural Case Studies*. Maryknoll, NY: Orbis.

The latter may feel particularly useful for pastoral workers as it is based on discussions of specific case examples.

Ethics and Pastoral Practice

As noted in the Introduction to this book, the literature on ethics specifically relating to pastoral care is not extensive. What literature there is often takes the form of journal articles rather than full-length books, and readers may find it useful to search journals such as the *Journal of Pastoral Care*, *Contact: The Interdisciplinary Journal of Pastoral Studies*, the *Journal of Psychology and Christianity* and the *Journal of Empirical Theology* for relevant material.

Don Browning's (1983) book *Religious Ethics and Pastoral Care* (Philadelphia: Fortress) is an important text in this area, though hard to obtain copies of. One of the main texts in this subject area still in print is Rebekah Miles' (1999) *The Pastor as Moral Guide* (Minneapolis: Fortress). Miles' approach is quite different (and theologically more conservative) to the one I have adopted here, and some readers might find it a useful complement to my text.

More Advanced Texts

Moving on from introductory level texts, there is again an extensive literature that gives a more advanced theoretical discussion of moral reflection. A range of more complex texts offer important discussions of what it means to 'do ethics' in our contemporary cultural and theological context. Good examples of such books are:

Bauman, Z. (1993) *Postmodern Ethics*. Oxford: Blackwell.
Hauerwas, S. (2001) *Naming the Silences: God, Medicine and the Problem of Suffering*. Edinburgh: T&T Clark.
MacIntyre, A. (1997) *After Virtue: A Study in Moral Theory*. Notre Dame: University of Notre Dame Press.
Stout, J. (2001) *Ethics After Babel*. Princeton: Princeton University Press.

Two advanced texts that explore the significance of values and moral reflection in relation to pastoral or religious practice are:

Browning, D. (1996) *A Fundamental Practical Theology*. Philadelphia: Fortress.
Graham, E. (1996) *Transforming Practice: Pastoral Theology in an Age of Uncertainty*. London: Mowbray.

Final Comment

The range of books listed above represents a helpful resource in terms of developing a broader awareness of issues in the field of ethics. What these books do not always do, however, is provide stimulating or engaging discussions of the nature of the good life. Indeed some of the best material to stimulate our thinking on what it means to live well can be found not in academic books on ethics, but in TV programmes, films and novels.

Engaging with contemporary ideas of the good life will therefore mean thinking critically about a whole range of popular cultural representations and explorations of what it means to live well from TV programmes such as *South Park* and *Sex in the City*, to films such as *The Matrix* and *Moulin Rouge*, to novels such as *Captain Corelli's Mandolin* and *Bridget Jones' Diary*. Some of the most accessible and creative current thinking about the good life can be found in these popular cultural forms and can be as valuable as resources for our ongoing thinking as the more academic or theoretical texts.

Bibliography

Adams, C. & Fortune, M. (1995) *Violence Against Women and Children: A Christian Theological Sourcebook*. New York: Continuum.

Argyris, C. & Schon, D. (1974) *Theory in Practice: Increasing Professional Effectiveness*. San Franscisco: Jossey-Bass.

Aristotle (2000) *Nichomachean Ethics* (translated and edited by R. Crisp). Cambridge: Cambridge University Press.

Arrington, R. (1999) *Western Ethics: An Historical Introduction*. Oxford: Blackwell.

Atkinson, D. (1994) *Pastoral Ethics*. London: Lynx.

Bauman, Z. (2000) *Liquid Modernity*. Cambridge: Polity.

Bellah, R., Madsen, R., Sullivan, W., Suidler, A. & Tipton, S. (1985) *Habits of the Heart: Individualism and Commitment in American Life*. Berkeley: University of California Press.

Bennett Moore, Z. (2001) 'The centrality of love: "pastoral" theology or "practical" theology – what's in a word?', paper presented at the annual conference of the *British and Irish Association for Practical Theology*, 17–19 July 2001, St Stephen's House, Oxford.

Bloomquist, K. (1989) 'Sexual violence: patriarchy's offense and defense,' in J. Brown & C. Bohn (eds), *Christianity, Patriarchy and Abuse*, Cleveland: Pilgrim Press, pp. 62–9.

Blytheway, B. (1995) *Ageism*. Buckingham: Open University Press.

Bohn, C. (1989) 'Dominion to rule: the roots and consequences of a theology of ownership,' in J. Brown & C. Bohn (eds), *Christianity, Patriarchy and Abuse*, Cleveland: Pilgrim Press, pp. 105–16.

Bond, J. & Coleman, P. (1993) 'Ageing into the Twenty-First Century,' in J. Bond, P. Coleman & S. Peace (eds), *Ageing in Society: An Introduction to Social Gerontology*, second edition, pp. 333–50.

Boyd, A. & Lynch, G. (1999) 'Establishing the therapeutic frame in pastoral settings,' in G. Lynch (ed.), *Clinical Counselling in Pastoral Settings*, London: Routledge, pp. 64–78.

British Association for Counselling and Psychotherapy (2001) *Code of Ethics and Practice for Counsellors*, downloaded from www.bac.co.uk, 11/10/01.

Broadus, L. (1996) 'Sex and violence in the family and church,' in E. Stuart et al (eds), *Christian Perspectives on Sexuality and Gender*, Grad Rapids, Mich.: Gracewing, pp. 400–9.

Browning, D. (1976) *The Moral Context of Pastoral Care*. Philadelphia: Fortress Press.

Browning, D. (1983) *Religious Ethics and Pastoral Care*. Philadelphia: Fortress Press.

Browning, D. (1987) *Religious Thought and the Modern Psychologies*. Philadelphia: Fortress.

Browning, D. (1988) 'The pastoral counselor as ethicist', *Journal of Pastoral Care*, vol. 42, 283–96.

Browning, D. (1991) *A Fundamental Practical Theology*. Minneapolis, Minn.: Fortress.

Bruce, S. (1995) *Religion in Modern Britain*. Oxford: Oxford University Press.

Brueggeman, W. (1993) *The Bible and Postmodern Imagination*. London: SCM

Campbell, A. (1984) *Moderated Love: A Theology of Professional Care*. London: SPCK.

Casement, P. (1985) *On Learning from the Patient*. London: Routledge.

Casement, P. (1990) *Further Learning from the Patient*. London: Routledge.

Cashman, H. (1993) *Christianity and Child Sex Abuse*. London: Darton, Longman and Todd.

Childs, B. (1990) *Short-Term Pastoral Counseling*. Nashville: Abingdon.

Cicero (1971) *On the Good Life*. Harmondsworth: Penguin.

Clebsch, W. & Jaekle, C. (1967) *Pastoral Care in Historical Perspective*. New York: Harper & Row.

Clinebell, H. (1984) *Basic Types of Pastoral Care and Counselling*. London: SCM.

Cooper, L. (1999) *Rousseau, Nature and the Problem of the Good Life*. University Park, Pennsylvania: Pennsylvania University Press.

Countryman, W. (1989) *Dirt, Greed and Sex*. London: SCM.

Davis, C. (1996) *Levinas: An Introduction*. Cambridge: Polity.

Diocese of Oxford (1996) *Code of Ministerial Practice*. Oxford: Oxford Diocese Office of Communications.

Ferrara, A. (1993) *Modernity and Authenticity: A Study of the Social and Ethical Thought of Jean-Jacques Rousseau*. New York: State University of New York Press.

Fletcher, J. (1966) *Situation Ethics*. London: SCM.

Frankena, W. (1973) *Ethics* (2nd edition). London: Prentice-Hall.

Foskett, J. & Lyall, D. (1988) *Helping the Helpers: Supervision and Pastoral Care*. London: SPCK.

Furniss, G. (1995) *Sociology for Pastoral Care*. London: SPCK.

Garma, J. (1991) 'A cry of anguish: the battered woman', in M. Glaz & J. Stevenson Moessner (eds), *Women in Travail and Transition*, Minneapolis: Fortune Press, pp. 126–45.

Gellner, E. (1985) *The Psychoanalytic Movement*. London: Palladin.

Gerkin, C. (1991) *Prophetic Pastoral Practice: A Christian Vision of Life Together*. Nashville: Abingdon.

Gergen, K. (1991) *The Saturated Self*. New York: Basic Books.

Gergen, K. (1994) *Realities and Relationships*. Cambridge, MA: Harvard University Press.

Goffman, E. (1961) *Asylums*. London: Penguin.

Gramsci, A. (1996) *Prison Letters*, translated by Hamish Henderson. London: Pluto.

Gray, A. (1994) *An Introduction to the Therapeutic Frame*. London: Routledge.

Green, M. & Holloway, R. (1980) *The Church and Homosexuality*. London: Hodder & Stoughton.

Hauerwas, S. (1981) *A Community of Character: Toward a Constructive Christian Social Ethic*. Notre Dame: University of Notre Dame Press.

Hauerwas, S. (1983) *The Peaceable Kingdom: A Primer in Christian Ethics*. London: SCM.

Hauerwas, S. (2001) *Naming the Silences: God, Medicine and the Problem of Suffering*. Edinburgh: T&T Clark.

Hoffman, J. (1979) *Ethical Confrontation in Counseling*. Chicago: University of Chicago Press.

Howe, D. (1993) *On Being a Client*. London: Sage.

Hurding, R. (1998) *Pathways to Wholeness: Pastoral Care in a Postmodern Age*. London: Hodder & Stoughton.

Jacobs, M. (1993) *Still Small Voice*. London: SPCK.

Johnson, J. (1995) 'Church response to domestic violence,' in C. Adams & M. Fortune (eds), *Violence Against Women and Children: A Christian Theological Sourcebook*. New York: Continuum, pp. 412–21.

Johnson, J. & Bondurant, D. (1995) 'Revisiting the 1982 Church response survey,' in C. Adams & M. Fortune (eds), *Violence Against Women and Children: A Christian Theological Sourcebook*. New York: Continuum, pp. 422–27.

Kagan, N. (1990) 'IPR – a validated model for the 1990s and beyond,' *Counseling Psychologist*, 18, 436–40.

Kantor, G. & Jasinski, J. (1998) 'Dynamics and risk factors in partner violence,' in J. Jasinski & L. Williams (eds), *Partner Violence: A Comprehensive Review of 20 Years of Research*, London: Sage, pp. 1–43.

Kelly, L. (1996) 'When does the speaking profit us? Reflections on the challenges of developing feminist perspectives on abuse and violence by women,' in M. Hester, L. Kelly & J. Radford (eds), *Women, Violence and Male Power*, Buckingham: Open University Press, pp. 34–49.

Keown, D. (2000) *Buddhism: A Very Short Introduction*. Oxford: Oxford University Press.

Lartey, E. (1997) *In Living Colour: An Intercultural Approach to Pastoral Care and Counselling*. London: Cassell.

Lartey, E. (2000) 'Practical theology as a theological form,' in S. Pattison & J. Woodward (eds), *The Blackwell Reader in Pastoral and Practical Theology*, Oxford: Blackwell, pp. 128–34.

Lasch, C. (1984) *The Minimal Self: Psychic Survival in Troubled Times*. New York: Norton.

Layzell, R. (1999) 'Pastoral counselling with those who have experienced abuse in religious settings,' in G. Lynch (ed.), *Clinical Counselling in Pastoral Settings*, London: Routledge, pp. 107–23.

Leech, K. (1994) *Soul Friend: Spiritual Direction in the Modern World*. London: Darton Longman & Todd.

Lomas, P. (1985) 'Who I am to teach morals?', in W. Dryden (ed.) *Therapist's Dilemmas*, London: Harper & Row, pp. 91–102.

Lyall, D. (1995) *Counselling in the Pastoral and Spiritual Context*. Milton Keynes: Open University Press.

Lynch, G. (1995) 'Moral reflection and the Christian pastoral counsellor,' *Contact: The Interdisciplinary Journal of Pastoral Studies*, vol. 117, 3–9.

Lynch, G. (1999a) 'A pragmatic approach to clinical counselling in context,' in J. Lees (ed.), *Clinical Counselling in Context: An Introduction*, London: Routledge, pp. 20–33.

Lynch, G. (1999b) 'Dual relationships in pastoral counselling,' in G. Lynch (ed.), *Clinical Counselling in Pastoral Settings*, London: Routledge, pp. 79–93.

MacIntyre, A. (1985) *After Virtue: A Study in Moral Theory* (2nd edition). London: Duckworth.

McFague, S. (1987) *Models of God: Theology for an Ecological Nuclear Age*. London: SCM.

McLeod, J. (1990) 'The client's experience of counselling: a review of the research literature,' in D. Mearns & W. Dryden (eds), *Experiences of Counselling in Action*, London: Sage, pp. 1–19.

McLeod, J. & Lynch, G. (2000) '"This is our life": strong evaluation in psychotherapy narrative,' *The European Journal of Psychotherapy, Counselling and Health*, 3: 3, 389–406.

Malby, B. & Pattison, S. (1999) *Living Values in the NHS: Stories from the NHS's 50th Year*. London: King's Fund.

Menzies Lyth, I. (1988) *Containing Anxiety in Institutions: Selected Essays*. London: Free Association.

Miles, R. (1999) *The Pastor as Moral Guide*. Minneapolis, Minn.: Fortress Press.

Noyce, G. (1989) *The Minister as Moral Counselor*. Nashville: Abingdon.

Oden, T. (1984) *The Care of Souls in the Classic Tradition*. Philadelphia: Fortress Press.

Pahl, R. (2000) *On Friendship*. Cambridge: Polity.

Pattison, S. (1988) *A Critique of Pastoral Care*. London: SCM.

Pattison, S. (1994) *Pastoral Care and Liberation Theology*. Cambridge: Cambridge University Press.

Pattison, S. (1997) *The Faith of the Managers*. London: Cassell.

Pattison, S. (1999) 'Are professional codes ethical?', *Counselling*, 10: 5, 374–80.

Pattison, S. (2000a) *Shame: Theory, Therapy, Theology*. Cambridge: Cambridge University Press.

Pattison, S. (2000b) 'Some straw for the bricks: a basic introduction to theological reflection', in S. Pattison & J. Woodward (eds), *The Blackwell Reader in Pastoral and Practical Theology*, Oxford: Blackwell, pp. 135–45.

Pattison, S. (2001) 'Are nursing codes of practice ethical?', *Nursing Ethics*, 8 (1), 5–18.

Peperzak, A. (ed.) (1995) *Ethics as First Philosophy*. London: Routledge.

Peperzak, A. (ed.) (1996) *Emmanuel Levinas: Basic Philosophical Writings*. Bloomington: Indiana University Press.

Pilcher, J. (1995) *Age & Generation in Modern Britain*. Oxford: Oxford University Press.

Poling, J. (1991) *The Abuse of Power: A Theological Problem*. Nashville: Abingdon Press.

Porter, J. (1994) *The Recovery of Virtue: The Relevance of Aquinas for Christian Ethics*. London: SPCK.

Price, A. (1989) *Love and Friendship in Plato and Aristotle*. Oxford: Clarendon Press.

Procter-Smith, M. (1995) '"Reorganizing victimization": the intersection between liturgy and domestic violence,' in C. Adams and M. Fortune (eds), *Violence Against Women and Children: A Christian Theological Sourcebook*. New York: Continuum, pp. 428–43.

Radford Ruether (1989) 'The Western religious tradition and violence against women in the home,' in J. Brown & C. Bohn (eds), *Christianity, Patriarchy and Abuse*, Cleveland: Pilgrim Press, pp. 31–40.

Reed, M. (1992) *The Sociology of Organizations: Themes, Perspectives and Prospects*. New York: Harvester Wheatsheaf.

Rogers, C. (1951) *Client-Centered Therapy*. Boston: Houghton Mifflin.

Rogers, C. (1961) *On Becoming a Person*. London: Constable.

Rogers, C. (1980) *A Way of Being*. Boston: Houghton Mifflin.

Rorty, R. (1999) *Philosophy and Social Hope*. London: Penguin.

Russell, J. (1993) *Out of Bounds: Sexual Exploitation in Counselling and Therapy*. London: Sage.

Rutter, P. (1989) *Sex in the Forbidden Zone*. New York: Harper & Row.

Sartre, J-P. (1973) *Existentialism and Humanism*. London: Methuen.

Schon, D. (1991a) *Educating the Reflective Practitioner*. San Francisco: Jossey-Bass.

Schon, D. (1991b) *The Reflective Practitioner: How Professionals Think in Action*. Aldershot: Ashgate.

Selby, P. (1983) *Liberating God: Private Care and Public Struggle*. London: SPCK.

Sennett, R. (1986) *The Fall of Public Man*. London: Faber & Faber.

Silverman, D. (1997) *Discourses of Counselling: HIV Counselling as Social Interaction*. London: Sage.

Smith, D. (1980) 'The concept of the good life', in D. Depew (ed.), *The Greeks and The Good Life*, Fullerton: California State University Press, pp. 17–32.

Spence, D. (1982) *Narrative Truth and Historical Truth*. New York: Norton.

Stott, J. (1990) *Issues Facing Christians Today* (2nd edition). London: Marshall Pickering.

Stuart, E. (1995) *Just Good Friends: Towards a Lesbian and Gay Theology of Relationships*. London: Mowbray.

Taylor, C. (1991) *The Ethics of Authenticity*. Cambridge, MA.: Harvard University Press.

Vardy, P. & Grosch, P. (1994) *The Puzzle of Ethics*. London: Fount.

Vitz, P. (1994) *Psychology as Religion* (Second edition). Exeter: Paternoster Press.